# Faith and Saving Faith

### Gordon H. Clark

The Trinity Foundation
Jefferson, Maryland

First edition © 1983 The Trinity Foundation
Second edition © 1990 The Trinity Foundation
Post Office Box 700
Jefferson, Maryland 21755

Printed in the United States of America.
ISBN 0-940931-95-8

# CONTENTS

## Books by Gordon H. Clark

*Readings in Ethics* (1931)
*Selections from Hellenistic Philosophy* (1940)
*A History of Philosophy* (coauthor, 1941)
*A Christian Philosophy of Education* (1946, 1988)
*A Christian View of Men and Things* (1952)
*What Presbyterians Believe* (1956)[1]
*Thales to Dewey* (1957, 1989)
*Dewey* (1960)
*Religion, Reason and Revelation* (1961, 1986)
*William James* (1963)
*Karl Barth's Theological Method* (1963)
*The Philosophy of Science and Belief in God* (1964, 1987)
*What Do Presbyterians Believe?* (1965, 1985)
*Peter Speaks Today* (1967)[2]
*The Philosophy of Gordon H. Clark* (1968)
*Biblical Predestination* (1969)[3]
*Historiography: Secular and Religious* (1971)
*II Peter* (1972)[2]
*The Johannine Logos* (1972, 1989)
*Three Types of Religious Philosophy* (1973, 1989)
*First Corinthians* (1975)
*Colossians* (1979, 1989)
*Predestination in the Old Testament* (1979)[3]
*I and II Peter* (1980)
*Language and Theology* (1980)
*First John* (1980)
*God's Hammer: The Bible and Its Critics* (1982, 1987)
*Behaviorism and Christianity* (1982)
*Faith and Saving Faith* (1983, 1990)
*In Defense of Theology* (1984)
*The Pastoral Epistles* (1984)
*The Biblical Doctrine of Man* (1984)
*The Trinity* (1985)
*Logic* (1985, 1988)
*Ephesians* (1985)
*Clark Speaks From the Grave* (1986)
*Logical Criticisms of Textual Criticism* (1986)
*First and Second Thessalonians* (1986)
*Predestination* (1987)
*The Atonement* (1987)
*The Incarnation* (1988)

[1] Revised in 1965 as *What Do Presbyterians Believe?*
[2] Combined in 1980 as *I & II Peter.*
[3] Combined in 1987 as *Predestination.*

# FOREWORD

Long before the neo-orthodox theologians thought of saying that faith is an encounter with a divine person rather than assent to a proposition, preachers who ought to have known better taught that faith is trust in a person, not belief in a creed. Years later, this writer, when a teen-ager, was told that some people would miss heaven by twelve inches—the distance between the head and the heart—because they believed the Gospel with their heads but not with their hearts. Today it is easier for a camel to pass through the eye of a needle than it is to find a minister—a conservative minister—who does not believe and teach that one must have a "personal" relationship with Christ in order to be saved. But what that "personal" relationship consists of is either not made explicit or, when made explicit, contradicts what the Bible teaches about saving faith. The result is that both Christians and non-Christians are either needlessly confused or totally misled. Perhaps the world is not responding to our message because the message is garbled. Neither we, nor they, know exactly what they must do to have eternal life.

Statements such as these about the head and the heart and trusting a person, not believing a creed, are not only false, they have created the conditions for the emergence of all sorts of religious subjectivism, from modernism to the charismatic movement and beyond. No one will miss heaven by twelve inches, for there is no distance between the head and the heart: "As a man thinks in his heart, so is he." The head/heart contrast is a figment of modern secular psychology, not a doctrine of divine revelation. St. Sigmund, not St. John, controls the pulpit in all too many churches.

Further, "trust in a person" is a meaningless phrase unless it means assenting to certain propositions about a person, propositions such as "I believe in God the Father Almighty . . . and in Jesus Christ his only Son, our Lord, who was conceived by the Holy Ghost, born of the Virgin Mary, suffered under Pontius Pilate, was crucified, dead, and buried; the third day he rose again from the dead; he ascended into heaven, and sits on the right hand of God the Father Almighty; from thence he shall come to judge the living and the dead." Trust in Christ, unless it means belief of these propositions, is totally without value. "Christ" *means* these propositions—and a lot more, to be sure, but at least these. No one who trusts in the Christs of Barth, Brunner, Renan or Tillich will be saved.

As for having a "personal" relationship with Christ, if the phrase means something more than assenting to true propositions about Jesus, what is that something more? Feeling warm inside? Coffee has the same effect. Surely "personal" relationship does not mean what we mean when we say that we know someone personally: Perhaps we have shaken his hand, visited his home or he ours, or eaten with him. John had a "personal" relationship with Christ in that sense, as did all the disciples, including Judas. But millions of Christians have not, and Jesus called them blessed: They have not seen and yet have believed. The difference between Judas and the other disciples is not that they had a "personal" relationship with Jesus and he did not, but that they believed, that is, assented to certain propositions about Jesus, while Judas did not believe those propositions. Belief of the truth, nothing more and nothing less, is what separates the saved from the damned. Those who maintain that there is something more than belief, are, quite literally, beyond belief.

In the pages that follow, Dr. Clark defends the view that faith is assent to a proposition, and that saving faith is assent to propositions found in the Bible. Saving faith is neither an indescribable encounter with a divine person, nor heart knowledge as opposed to head knowledge. According to the author of Hebrews, those who come to God must believe at least two propositions: That he is, and that he is a rewarder of them that diligently seek him. Mindless encounters and meaningless relationships are not saving faith. Truth is propositional, and one is saved and sanctified only through believing true statements. Faith comes by hearing, and hearing by the Word of God.

The anti-intellectual cast of virtually all modern thought, from the university chair to the barroom stool, controls the pulpits as well. It is this pious anti-intellectualism that emphasizes encounter rather than information, emotion instead of understanding, "personal" relationship rather than knowledge. But Christians, Paul wrote, have the mind of Christ. Our relationship to him is intellectual. And since Christ *is* his mind and we are ours, no relationship could be more intimate than that. That is precisely why the Scriptures use the analogy of marriage to illustrate the intellectual relationship between Christians and Christ.

This recognition of the primacy of the intellect, the primacy of truth, is totally missing from contemporary theology. One of this century's greatest theologians and writers, J. Gresham Machen, wrote a book entitled *What Is Faith?* fifty years ago. His words are as appropriate today as they were then:

This anti-intellectual tendency in the modern world is no trifling thing; it has its roots deep in the entire philosophical development of modern times. Modern philosophy . . . has had as its dominant note, certainly as its present day result, a depreciation of the reason and a skeptical answer to Pilate's question, "What is truth?" This attack upon the intellect has been conducted by men of marked intellectual powers; but an attack it has been all the same. And at last the logical results of it, even in the sphere of practice, are beginning to appear. A marked characteristic of the present day is a lamentable intellectual decline, which has appeared in all fields of human endeavor excpet those that deal with purely material things. The intellect has been browbeaten so long in theory that one cannot be surprised if it is now ceasing to function in practice . . .

As over against this anti-intellectual tendency in the modern world, it will be one chief purpose of the present little book to defend the primacy of the intellect, and in particular to try to break down the false and disastrous opposition which has been set up between knowledge and faith.

That, too, is a chief purpose of this little book. The following pages argue that it is rational to believe what God says; it is irrational to disbelieve God. No argument is more urgently needed than that.

John W. Robbins
President

January 31, 1983
Jefferson, Maryland

# PREFACE

The motivation for this study of the nature of faith is the edification of Christians: "Let all things be done for edification" (I Corinthians 14:26). More specifically this book is addressed to conservative-minded, orthodox, evangelical, Bible-believing Protestants.

Naturally the author would be happy to have some secularists read it too. Most of them are so uninformed as to the theology of the Protestant Reformation that their remarks on religion just about qualify as bigotry. The presidential campaign of 1980, on one side, virtually tried to reduce Bible-believing Christians to the status of second class citizens, or worse.

But the people to whom this material is addressed merit some castigation too. Many of them think that secularists have nothing worthwhile to offer. One should by all means preach the gospel to them with the hope that in their darkness they may see a great light; but the idea that anti-christian philosophers can actually help Christians to understand the Bible is anathema.

However, contemporary evangelicalism has deteriorated so greatly from the theological achievements of the sixteenth and seventeenth centuries that one might suppose it has reverted to the Romish views of an "implicit" faith of unknown content.

Therefore whatever small literary skill this author may

have developed during his teaching career has here been
defaced both by some extremely elementary Scriptural exegesis and also by constant reminders that Christians should pay a
certain amount of attention to secular scholars. The secular
material itself not only impinges on New Testament teaching,
but is really very interesting, at least to a theologian; and to
every patient reader it will prove edifying.

# 1. Introduction

The thief on the cross said, "Lord, remember me;" and Jesus replied, "Today thou shalt be with me in paradise." After a life of crime one of the three worst criminals in the nation— Barabbas had been released—this thief received assurance of heaven.

He could hardly have known much about Jesus. He certainly had no notion of saving faith, let alone of the Trinity, the Atonement, or the second advent. Yet, on the authority of Jesus, we know that he was saved. Is it necessary then to have saving faith, or faith of any kind? Must we know what saving faith is? Does one have to read the Bible and listen to evangelistic sermons? What is the relation between faith and knowledge? Surely entrance into heaven does not require a degree from a theological seminary. The thief was saved in ignorance.

However, let us not exaggerate. Very probably, indeed certainly, the thief knew more than most people think he did. For one thing, he knew the charge on which Christ had been condemned. Even if he had been so illiterate that he could not have read the inscription on Christ's cross, he could not help hearing the screams of the crowd as they ridiculed Christ's claim to be King, Savior, and God. He also knew the charge on which he himself had been condemned. He had lived a life of serious crime, and now he acknowledged that his condemnation and execution were just. In reply to the other thief's participation in ridiculing Jesus, he said, "Do you not even fear

God, since you are under the same sentence of condemnation? And we indeed justly, for we are receiving what we deserve for our deeds." Not only did he fear God and admit his guilt, but he added, "This man has done nothing wrong." How did he know that Jesus had done nothing wrong? Being such an enterprising criminal and cognizant of the daily news from the cities and villages, he must have heard rumors about this itinerant preacher. As Christ preached to the multitudes, the thief might have been picking their pockets and also picking up some few ideas of what Christ was saying. We must therefore not under-estimate the extent of the thief's knowledge; but we can be pretty sure that he had no theological theory about the nature of saving faith.

Even knowing so little the thief compares favorably with some Americans today. They do not know they are guilty, nor do they fear God. Some do not even believe there is a God. Then there is one thing the thief knew which hardly any Ameri-can knows. He knew he would die within a few hours. Our contemporaries, comfortably ensconced before their TV's, do not have such sombre expectations. When we stop to think, we see that the thief knew more than we first suspected. But all in all; he still did not know very much.

If now he got to heaven without much knowledge, why should we bother to examine the psychology of saving faith or trouble ouselves with theological investigations? If knowledge is indeed required, a very little will suffice. If we do not know what it means to believe, still we believe and are saved.

However, that one piece of knowledge which the thief had and which we do not have prevents us from taking him as a norm for our action. He knew he would be dead before night-fall. We do not. He had no opportunity of living a Christian life. We do. To suppose that ignorance is sufficient for a Christian life is to be ignorant of what a Christian life requires.

Remember that Christ said, "Make disciples of all the nations
. . . teaching them to observe all that I commanded you." The
thief on the cross, and anyone else who is on his death-bed, is
excused from obeying this commandment. But the rest of us
are not. We are obliged to teach, and before we can teach, we
must learn—learn all, or all we can, of what Christ himself
taught and what he taught through his disciples. Remember
also that *all* Scripture has been breathed out by God and that it
is *all* profitable for teaching. But we cannot teach the Christian
message without first learning it. This small book endeavors to
explain what the New Testament teaches about faith.

## 2. Generic Faith: Brand Blanshard

This small book, as was just said, aims to expound what
the New Testament, and the Bible as a whole, says about saving
faith. But saving faith is a species of faith in general. Faith is
not limited to Christian faith. Jewish faith, Islamic faith, and
even secular faiths are faith. Not only Christian theologians,
but secular philosophers also have been interested in and have
written about faith. Some small acquaintance with their views
will prove profitable, even if only by sharp contrast, in understanding Christian faith. The devout Christian reader expects,
and will not be disappointed, to find a great deal of Biblical
material in this study. In fact, the Bible is the main source and
only authority. Nevertheless a few pages on one or two secular
views make a good preliminary section.

First, let us consider Brand Blanshard's *The Nature of
Thought*,[1] (Vol. I. pp.112ff.) because in it we also find the views
of two other secular thinkers. His first remarks are rather

---

1. George Allen & Unwin Ltd., 1939.

discouraging: "What is ordinarily meant when we say we believe something? One may reply that it is an acceptance or conviction or adoption or affirmation or mental assertion of some proposition; but these are all synonyms, not definitions. The fact is that belief, central as it is in the life of thought, and perhaps because it *is* so essential, is indefinable and probably indescribable."

A most patient and persistent attempt to explain belief, according to Blanshard, was that of the Wurzburg school. One of them reduced belief to an indescribable *Bewusstseinslage* (contents of consciousness or awareness), neither determinate ideas nor volitions. Another used the phrase "a content image-lessly present as knowledge." A third spoke of an intellectual attitude which "may be a glow or halo of indescribable con-sciousness." Others said similar things.

For the benefit of the Christian reader who knows little about the history of psychology and is anxious to arrive at a Biblical view of the matter, it may be suggested that view number two may be of some help, but that the others are of little value for anything.

Not all psychologists were as disappointing as the Wurz-burgers. Bertrand Russell was somewhat more definite. Russell was of course a vigorous enemy of Christianity; further-more he changed his opinions rather often; nevertheless, his view of belief is a background against which a Christian must work. "The content of a belief," says Russell, "may consist of words only, or of images only, or of a mixture of the two, or either or both together with one or more sensations. . . . In this [latter] case your belief consists of a sensation and an image suitably related."

On this section, not given here in full, Blanshard remarks, "Now a rough count discloses in this passage some fifteen distinguishable propositions, of which one seems to me true, one doubtful, and thirteen false." Obviously, therefore, secular philosophers disagree considerably as to the nature of belief. Though none of them is interested in defending Christianity, Christians might nonetheless find some worthwhile suggestions as to the nature of faith. The material certainly offers us a wide choice.

This welter of conflicting opinions, continues Blanshard, "tends to support the view of James that belief is 'perfectly distinct, but perfectly indescribable in words,' that 'it feels like itself—and that is about as much as we can say.' However [still Blanshard] this is not quite all we can say. We can say that belief is *not* sensation, that it is *not the use of words or images, though these may accompany it, and that it is not* the same as desire or feeling. . . . James, to be sure, thinks it *is* a feeling, and speaks of those states of intoxication in which a man's soul will sweat with conviction and he be all the while unable to tell what he is convinced of at all."

Unfortunately, at least in the present writer's opinion, many Christians, motivated by an irrational pragmatism or by an even more extremely irrational mysticism, consider belief to be an emotion or feeling. To be sure, some beliefs stir the emotions, but the very sober belief that a man has five fingers on each hand is as much a belief as some shattering bad news. Nor can believing good news, namely the Good News, be a mere emotion.

Blanshard appropriately notes that two Roman Catholic philosophers, Descartes and Newman, in different ways, made belief an act of will. He himself holds that this is too specific and definite—a strange criticism—but then he adds that belief is "virtually identical with mind on its intellectual side." As corroboration he quotes Mill: "Its distinctive character is such, Mill said, that 'when we arrive at it, we seem to have reached, as it were, the central point of our intellectual nature' which all other functions presuppose." In defense of this proposition he adduces the following instance. "How important belief is for perception may be made clear by considering (1) that if in perceiving an orange our thought were confined to what we see, we should remain penned in a coloured patch and never arrive at an orange at all, and (2) that to say, as some writers do, that we should even see a coloured patch is, strictly, wrong. One can no doubt see a colour, but at the level at which one apprehends a coloured patch, rudimentary judgement is present. To talk of 'sensing *patches* of colour,' except by way of metonomy, is to talk loosely; no patch could possibly be sensed."

College students, bank tellers, and many Christian apologists exhibit surprised disbelief that one cannot sense a patch of color. What can possibly be more evident than that we see color? But Blanshard, independently arriving at a conclusion that St. Augustine long ago expressed, insists that adults, if not babies, can have no sensation of blue minus all intellectual interpretation. Here the serious reader should begin to consider what a sensation might be, and how, if there is such a thing, it can fit into a theory of learning.

Although Blanshard was not a Christian, he was not particularly motivated by anti-christian bias in these passages.[2] Therefore, it is just possible that some of his observations could

---

2. It is otherwise in his 620 page *Reason and Belief* (George Allen & Unwin, 1974). Here he uncritically reproduces the mistakes of Moses in the Ingersoll manner, the critical theories of Wellhausen on Jewish history, without mentioning these two names, and in general the destructive higher criticism. His exegesis is unconsidered and takes no account of conservative views. Two examples are the number of angels at the tomb Easter morning and the impossibility that God can be both one substance and three Persons. In addition to these "contradictions," which any Christian garage mechanic can handle, there is another one less well-known. In II Samuel 6:23 we read that Michal, the first wife of David, had no children to the day of her death; but in II Samuel 21:8 she is said to have borne five sons. Blanshard, to the detriment of his scholarly reputation, suppresses the evidence that some manuscripts of the latter verse read *Merab*, not Michal. Even the liberal Revised Standard Version prints *Merab*.

be incorporated into a Christian philosophy. At any rate, there are good orthodox Christian apologetes today who, in my opinion, teach nonsense because they are unacquainted with professional studies of sensation, mind, and belief. Even their relatively faithful biblical account of saving faith is defective because they do not understand faith *simpliciter*. The biblical account of saving faith presupposes a view of human nature, not merely as sinful, but as natural. The assertion that men believe falsehoods, being deceived by Satan, does not excuse the apologete from searching out the Biblical view of sensation, perception, intellection, volition, and belief.

## 3. Generic and Secular Belief: H.H. Price

In 1960 Professor H.H. Price delivered one of the Gifford Lecture series at the University of Aberdeen. These lectures, considerably expanded, were published by George Allen & Unwin in 1969, under the title *Belief*. Some thoughts from its 488 pages will serve as another example of how secular scholars treat the general subject of belief. Obviously no summary of the entire work is possible here.

The opening pages describe two contrasting methodologies between which, Price seems to say, every student of the problem must choose. The traditional method and the only method used until recently assumes that "believing is a special sort of mental occurrence (sometimes described as a 'mental' act . . . [which] need not necessarily be introspected by the person in whom it occurs; but it always *could* be . . . . The modern way of treating belief is quite different. Believing something is now generally regarded not as an occurrence . . . but as a disposition. . . . This is equivalent to a series of conditional statements describing what he *would* be likely to say or do or feel if such and such circumstances were to arise. For example, he would assert the proposition (aloud, or privately to himself) if he heard someone else denying it . . . . He would use it, when relevant, as a premise in his inferences . . . he would act as if it were true. If it were falsified he would feel surprised, and would feel no surprise if it were verified. . . . The occurrent believings or 'acts of believing' which the traditional theorists discussed are on this view mythical entities" (pp. 19-20).

Although Professor Price here pictures these two views as mutually exclusive, and although the adherents of the contemporary method do so also, for they refer to the traditional view as mythical, Price nonetheless hints that the traditional view can accommodate the later view even if the latter cannot accommodate the former. This non-reciprocal relationship is of some importance, as will be seen some pages further on. At the moment Price's hint can be expanded by saying that although believing something for many years may not be an instantaneous act, there must have been some such act when a person passes from ignorance, inattention, or even disbelief to a conscious acceptance of the proposition in question. The traditional analysis does not or need not deny that I believe two and two are four even when my mind is occupied with a chess problem or when I am asleep. The contemporary view sometimes makes use of prejudicial expressions. On page 189 Price says, "As Professor Ryle has pointed out, it sounds very odd indeed to say 'at half past three I was engaged in believing that Oxford would win the boat race.'" Price himself recognized the inappropriateness of Ryle's illustration and replies, "it does make sense to say that I assented to a proposition $p$ at half past three today." Does this then not permit us to say that philosophically the initial act of believing is the more important? Christians, who read "Believe on the Lord Jesus Christ, and thou shalt be saved," cannot minimize this initial act, no matter how useful it is to remember, on a later relevant occasion, that stuffed green peppers resulted in indigestion.

Perhaps these remarks relative to the first pages of Price's second lecture have pushed us a little too far forward. But the religious implication will return us to a noteworthy page in the first lecture. There Price makes an observation which this monograph also wishes to emphasize. Suppose someone says, "What difference does it make which of these two analyses of belief—if either—is the correct one? Who cares whether 'Jones believes that *p*' is or is not a purely dispositional statement about Mr. Jones? . . . My reply, however, is that in philosophy the longest way round is often the shortest way home. . . . If belief in a religious world-view is what interests us most, we shall be in a better position for considering this subject if we first pay some attention to the nature of belief in general" (pp. 23-24). Price mentions one specific example of the coincidence of the secular and the religious problem: it is "the distinction between believing 'in' and believing 'that' " (p. 348). We may both believe *that* the president has wisely vetoed a bill, and, or, we may believe *in* the president. Pilate seems to have believed *that* Jesus was innocent, but he did not believe *in* Jesus. There must be some distinction between these two beliefs, whether their object is the president or Jesus. What is this distinction? If we mistake the difference, the result to ourselves will be more serious in the latter case than in the former. The present monograph will, later on, pay particular and detailed attention to what the New Testament teaches on this point.

Another element in secular philosophy which reappears in religious discussions, or rather an element discussed in religion for centuries before Bertrand Russell and others latched on to it, is the alleged distinction between knowledge by "acquaintance" and knowledge by "description." Price, loquaciously enough to justify the omission of several phrases, writes as follows: "Various sorts of dependent clauses . . . follow the verb 'to know.' But sometimes it is not followed by a dependent clause at all. Instead, it governs an accusative—a noun or a noun phrase. We speak of knowing Mr. Robertson Smith . . . or Kensington Gardens. . . . This is very different from 'knowledge that' " (p. 50).

The importance of this distinction, or, more accurately, the importance of deciding whether or not there is such a distinction, is considerable, and the devout non-philosophical Christian can hardly suspect at this point how important it is for understanding John's Gospel.

Price continues: " 'Knowledge that' may be called a 'propositional attitude.' But the knowledge we are now discussing is not a propositional attitude at all. It is sometimes called knowledge by acquaintance. One cannot have it unless one has actually encountered [by sensory perception?] the person or thing which is known. . . . Perhaps we cannot know anything by acquaintance without coming to know at least some facts or truths about it. But certainly we can know truths or facts about something without being acquainted with it. . . . Students of Roman History may know many facts about Julius Caesar, but they are not in a position to know *him*."

The Christian must now ask himself, Can one know Jesus Christ with the knowledge of acquaintance, that is to say, by sensory perception? Or is our knowledge of Christ merely unimportant knowledge about him? Is "knowledge about" unimportant? Is there any knowledge that is not "knowledge about" ?

Price, to support the contention that there are two distinct types of knowledge, adduces the use, in some languages, of two different words for *know*: *cognoscere* and *scire, connaitre* and *savoir, kennen* and *wissen*. Price allows that English has now deleted this distinction. Price does not appeal to the Greek verbs *gignosko* versus *oida*. The use of these two verbs is much too confusing for Price's purpose. Liddell and Scott report *gignosko* (same root as the Latin *cognoscere*) as "come to know, perceive, and in past tenses *know* with the accusative; as distinct from *oida* know by reflection, *gignosko* = know by observation." But then the lexicon adds a most interesting instance from Aristotle's *Posterior Analytics:* "It is difficult to know (*gnonai*) if one knows (*oiden*) or not; for it is difficult to know (*gnonai*) whether or not we know (*ismen*) by means of the first principles in each case" (76 a 26-27). *Ismen* is the first person indicative plural of *oida.* It is a second perfect of *eidon,* to see, related to the Latin *video.* Under *eido* Liddell and Scott give "see, perceive, . . . before the eyes, . . . experience, . . . see mentally, perceive . . . examine, investigate, . . . consider. . . . *oida* I see with the mind's eye, i.e., I know . . . The aorist and perfect are usually supplied by *gignosko* . . . be acquainted with, . . . one acquainted with the fact . . . with knowing mind . . . *ouk oid' ei* I know not whether. . . ."

Now try to explain Aristotle's meaning while observing Price's alleged distinction. Should we say, "It is difficult to know by reflection whether we perceive by the eyes"? Or if *oida* means to know by reflection and *gignosko* means to know by observation, as the lexicon said (see above), should we translate Aristotle as "It is difficult to know by observation whether we know by reflection"? Hardly: Aristotle seems to use the two verbs synonymously. If indeed Latin, German, and French made a systematic distinction, why cannot we say that the Greeks were more philosophic than the Latins and the later English discovered that the earlier Anglo-Saxon was confused? In recent days several philosophic authors have tried to base their theories on linguistic usage. The present writer does not approve. Price's statement that "In the examples mentioned earlier (knowing a person, or a country, or an object such as an oak tree) it was plausible to say that knowledge by acquaintance is not a propositional attitude at all" (p. 52), is a statement which, plausible as it may seem to some people, seems to at least one person to be definitely false.

To examine all the details that Professor Price adduces, nearly every one of which is intensely interesting, at least to a philosopher, would discourage some less professional readers. However, even the less professional should be warned that Price's reliance on the occurrence of sense data (e.g., pp. 57 ff.) is rejected by the neohegelian Blanshard as well as by the great Christian theologian St. Augustine. Locke insisted on sense data, and Kant, in a very different setting, spoke of *Das Gegebenes*, but the beginning student in philosophy must be warned that such is not a point of universal agreement. The subject is really quite complicated.

There is also another immediacy, often emphasized by contemporary conservative Christian apologetes. It is self-knowledge. Price says, "Surely each of us must know himself in some degree . . . We certainly do possess it" (p. 62). I acknowledge that Price adds some qualifications. But at the moment I merely want to cast doubt on the possibility of knowing one's self by quoting, "The heart is deceitful above all things and desperately wicked: who can know it?" The following verse suggests that only God knows a man. If now knowledge by acquaintance is an unintelligible phrase, equally unacceptable is Price's and Russell's description of knowledge by description. In both cases the *object* of knowledge is misconstrued. Further elucidation here of the object of knowledge would too much tax the reader's patience. The main point is to realize how complicated the subject matter actually is.

Price's book is detailed, complicated, and very interesting. At times it is disappointing. At one point, discussing Locke's theory of degrees of assent (p. 131), he says, "These doctrines of

Locke . . . may strike us as just obvious common sense." This phraseology does not bind Price to agreement with Locke, but they suggest that he does, for on the next page he adds, "Do we not all agree with Locke that a lower degree of assent may be justified when a higher degree would not be?" The answer to this rhetorical question is, No, we do not all agree, and Locke's view is not obvious "common sense." Price continues on the following page (p. 133) "Locke's two doctrines, then—that assent has degrees [here I am not interested in the second] may easily seem platitudinous." Granted that he immediately continues by discussing Cardinal Newman's contrary argument, he yet seems to accept Locke too easily. Indeed, he says, "I shall try to show that Locke is more nearly right than Newman." Later on (p. 204) he again mentions Locke's theory that assent has degrees; and throughout the book he seems to delight in describing minute differences in consciousness; yet on page 207 Price admits that "You cannot partially decide for $p$, or half choose it." And after some interesting description of our reactions to implausible news, he allows that "assent may be voluntary in the long run, at least sometimes, even though in the short run it is quite beyond our voluntary control" (p. 223).

Continuing this discussion of Newman many pages later, Price notes a fundamental blunder that nearly all Empiricists fall into. Pages 324-330 describe the unusually vivid imagery by which Newman carried on his thinking: not only visual imagery, but the other four types as well. Then Newman, like Hume[3], assumed that all people had similar imagery. Francis Galton, thirteen years after Newman's *Grammar of Assent*, in his *Inquiries into Human Faculty*, recorded empirical disproof of this assumption. Since the present writer is intimately

---

3. Compare my *Thales to Dewey*, (Jefferson, Maryland: The Trinity Foundation, 1989), pp. 382-384.

acquainted with one who has no such imagery at all, he considers all empiricism to be vitiated *ab initio*. This applies to Price as well as to Newman and Hume. Of course some things Price and Newman say are inconsistently true, or may be true by some adaptation, as when, for example, Price in a footnote on page 333 says "Newman seems to admit [that]. . . . Real assent is in itself an intellectual act."[4]

If some devout readers find these matters a little too far removed from religious importance, Price's next to last chapter can hardly fail to suggest that Christians can profit by such discussions. The title is, *Belief 'in' and Belief 'that.'*

On pages 426ff. Price notes that in religious circles *belief in* is of more interest than *belief that*. The latter is a more secular concept; and the devout insist that there is a great difference between them. Philosophers on the other hand usually think not and attempt to reduce *in* to *that*. However, as Price notes, even secularists use *belief-in*. A blind man believes-in his dog. Englishmen used to believe-in the British Empire. Some parents believe-in a liberal arts education for their children. Women's lib believes-in killing babies. Can these beliefs-in be reduced to beliefs-that? For example, belief *in* the Loch Ness monster simply means someone believes *that* there is such a creature. The Tories of the nineteenth century did not believe *in* Gladstone; that is, they did not believe *that* he was a good prime minister. But since a person who believes *in* God in the sense that there is a God may himself be irreligious, belief-in may seem to contain an irreducible factor.

Price thus concludes that belief-in has two senses, one

---

4. Read the literary gem, *The Passion for the Theoretical* (pp. 334-336). Price does not himself have the same enthusiasm he depicts in the mathematician and logician; but others do. May one add among these others the ideal theologian. By the time Price takes Newman to page 345, Newman seems to be an outright idolater. This is a constant danger in Romanism.

reducible and the other not (p. 435); but his argument is weak. He makes a distinction between factual beliefs and evaluative beliefs, yet he has a hard time finding an evaluation that cannot be expressed factually. Does not belief-in militarism, or in pacifism, reduce to belief-that factually it is profitable in one way or another? Price's opponents argue that the *object* of such a belief is an evaluation and we believe that the evaluation is correct. The difference between various beliefs lies in the objects or propositions believed, not in the nature of belief.

When Price begins to argue against the reduction of *belief in* to *belief that*, his line of thought becomes confused. Some of it is too trivial. For example, "to believe in my physician" cannot be reduced to "to believe that he is a morally good man," or that "he is good at water-colour painting:" he must be "good at curing diseases" (p. 442). Precisely: This triviality is a systematic confusion, for belief in my physician is obviously belief that he is a good doctor. Making much of the distinction between a factual belief and an evaluative belief, he repudiates the reduction on the ground that the one is not the other. This device, clearly, substitutes one proposition for another; the object of belief is changed, but changing the object of the belief does not indicate any theoretical difference between factual and evaluative beliefs. To believe-in a certain value, virtue for example, is to believe-that virtue is a value. The logic, the analysis, the nature of "All a is b" remains identical no matter what values are assigned to the two variables.

By such a confused procedure, Price finally concludes "Trusting is not a merely cognitive attitude. . . . The proposed reduction leaves out the 'warmth' which is a characteristic feature of evaluative belief-in. . . . If it is disagreeable to be compelled to talk about 'the heart,' the fact remains that most of us have one, as well as a head" (p. 452).

Later on the Biblical view of such a distinction between

the heart and the head must be stated. Here as this secular section comes to an end, one need note only that after pages and pages describing various beliefs, Price gives no explanation of his words *warmth, head,* or *heart.* The defect is major. He has solved his problem with meaningless words.

A technical point relative to this gap in Price's argument comes at the top of the same page: "Trusting is not merely a cognitive attitude." One need not reject this statement as false. Rather it is misapplied. No belief is a merely cognitive attitude. After spending so many pages on Newman's *Grammar of Assent,* Price should have considered the possibility that every belief is a volitional attitude, or volitional act. As such it has no bearing on the reducibility or irreducibility of *in* to *that.*

It should now be clear that secular analyses of belief are applicable to the same problem in Christian Theology. Some Scriptural material is as descriptive as Price's many pages; some is more analytical. The problem is identical, and we should not refuse to learn even from those with whom we are in basic disagreement.

There is one further lesson we may learn. Professor Price is so very honest that he does all he can to find some value in every view he discusses. The result is that every view becomes equally or almost equally questionable. If we, like him, were left to our own natural resources, we could have little confidence in any view. Though Price states some preferences, the whole gives an impression of skepticism. The more we study his arguments, the more this impression is reinforced. But we Christians do not claim to rely on our natural resources. We claim to have received a supernatural revelation. If we patiently study this revelation and carefully avoid illogicalities, we shall reach the truth, or at least some of it.

## 4. Roman Catholic Views

In the preceding section the material from Price included some of his remarks on Cardinal Newman. More needs to be said about Roman Catholic views. Perhaps we should refer to the Roman Catholic view in the singular, for the several writers are in substantial agreement. Hence we shall go back to Newman's source, Thomas Aquinas, and forward to the recent M.C. D'Arcy, S.J.

Since the early Christians, before A.D. 325, had not settled upon the doctrine of the Trinity, it is not surprising that they had no clear view of faith. Tertullian spoke about believing on authority rather than by personal investigation and knowledge. After Athanasius, Augustine had more to say. Faith for him was voluntary assent to the truth. This is more to the point than Tertullian's very good, but quite inadequate passages.

As one of the greatest thinkers in the history of philosophy and theology, Thomas Aquinas demands notice. Here a reference to a previous medieval theologian, Hugo St. Victor, will conveniently introduce the discussion. Hugo proposed a definition of faith that was widely accepted both before and after the Protestant Reformation: "Faith is a kind of certainty concerning absent realities that is superior to opinion and inferior to knowledge." This sort of division is reminiscent of the fine distinctions described by H.H. Price, which can be useful only if each is distinctly defined. Thomas, however, strikes deeper. He objects that a mean must always be homogeneous to its two extremes. Since both science and opinion have propositions as their objects, the objects of faith (which is intermediate between them) must likewise be propositions. Then Thomas, always willing to present an opponent's view, acknowledges that contrary to what he has just said, the Apostles' Creed asserts "I believe in God the Father Almighty," and this is different from the proposition, "God is Almighty." Therefore, echoing Hugo St. Victor, faith concerns a reality, not a proposition. Further, in heaven faith gives way to vision, as I Corinthians 13:12 says; and this is a vision of God himself, not a proposition; therefore similarly the object of faith is a person, not a proposition.

After stating opposing views Thomas does not always come down on one side as against the other. He sometimes effects a combination. Here, noting the divergency, he gives this conclusion in the *Summa Theologica* (Blackfriars edition, Vol. 31, pp. 11 ff.): "The way the known exists in the knower corresponds to the way the knower knows. . . . For this reason the human mind knows in a composite way things that are themselves simple. . . . From the perspective of the one believing, the object of faith is something composite in the form of a proposition. . . . In heaven . . . that vision will not take the form of a proposition, but of a simple intuition."

This quotation presents two and a half puzzles. First is the triviality, tautology, or vagary that the way the known exists in the knower corresponds to the way the knower knows. This does not describe what these ways are, and therefore leaves in doubt whether or not the way the knower knows is the way the object itself exists. The second and third, or second and a half puzzle, concerns the distinction between knowing in this life and knowing in heaven. If God is so simple as not to be a proposition, so simple as not to be a subject with predicates, how can he turn into a subject and predicate when he enters a human mind? Or otherwise, if our propositional knowledge of God be true, what becomes of this truth in heaven? Does it become false? Thomas says that God becomes a vision or simple intuition. *Vision*, however, as when Scripture says that we shall see him face to face, is clearly metaphorical, for God is not a visible body. And as for *intuition*, some philosophers have asserted the occurrence of intellectual intuitions, especially axiomatic propositions. It is hard to credit the idea that truth can be non-propositional. The single word *cat* is neither true nor false. The proposition, "this cat is black," may be true; but how can a subject minus a predicate be true all alone by itself? Yet God is the truth, and his mind, his omniscience, is the totality of all truths.

Another of Thomas' points is even more clearly implausible. He insists that we cannot believe anything that is false. To quote: "Nothing can be the completion of any potentiality . . . except in virtue of the formal objective of that power. For example, color cannot be the completion of sight except through light . . . . Nothing therefore can come under faith except in its status within God's truth, where nothing false has any place. . . . We can only conclude that nothing false can be the object of faith."

Such was not Augustine's view, and on the face of it St. Thomas' statement is just plain false. And if so, Thomas has believed a false proposition, which he said no one can do. People believe many false propositions. Augustine used as an example the belief of a boy that a certain man and woman were his parents, whereas he had actually been adopted soon after his birth.

This is so obvious that we must suppose Aquinas to have meant something else. If he had saving faith in mind, instead of faith in general, his statement would be true. Saving faith must be belief in something God has said, not something Herodotus or Celsus had said. Therefore the object of faith must be true and cannot be false. No one can be saved by believing a falsehood. But with this quite understandable meaning, the meaning of faith disappears. It reduces to a tautology, namely, faith can have no false statement as an object because we refuse the name *faith* to any belief that has a false statement as its object; and thus Thomas here gives no information as the nature of belief and its place in one's consciousness. Of course, this is not all St. Thomas said.

Some pages further on (Blackfriars' edition, p. 61) Thomas gives a fuller explanation: "The verb *to think* can be used in three senses. The first is the widest sense—any act of intellectual knowing. . . . The second is a narrower sense, where *thinking* designates a thinking of the mind that is accompanied by a certain searching prior to reaching complete understanding in the certitude of seeing. . . . The third sense is an act of the cogitative power [and has no part in this discussion.] . . . In its first and broadest sense, 'to think with assent' does not bring out the precise meaning. . . . If, however, *to think* is understood in its proper sense, the text does express the meaning distinctive of the act of belief. Among the acts of the intellect, some include a firm assent without pondering—thus when someone thinks about what he knows scientifically . . . Other mental acts are . . . inconclusive . . . suspicion . . . opinion. The act of believing, however, is firmly attached to one alternative, and in this respect the believer is in the same state of mind as one who has science or understanding."[5]

Since this is not a treatise on Thomistic philosophy and cannot therefore analyze the innumerable details, a rather summary conclusion, minus the niceties and requisite modifications, may be permitted. The last of the quoted sentences, identifying the believing state of mind with the scientific state of mind, more or less justifies the conclusion that faith, for Thomas, is an assent to an understood proposition. And to that extent we agree.

Somewhere in a discussion on faith, the Romish view of

5. The notes in the Blackfriars' edition list other passages that go into further details.

"implicit" faith should be considered. When an Italian or Irish peasant asserts that he believes whatever the Church teaches, though, of course, his knowledge of what the Church teaches embraces no more than one percent of the Tridentine confession, he is said to have implicit faith. Even an educated Catholic, a professor of philosophy in a secular university, did not know the essential element that makes baptism valid. But all such people profess belief in *whatever* the Church teaches. Protestantism has always rejected this proposition as absurd. It should be clear that no one can believe what he does not know or understand. Suppose a person who knows no French is told, "Dans ce roman c'est M. DuPrès qui est le meurtrier": can he believe it? If he could, it would greatly ease the work of foreign missionaries: they could preach to the Chinese or Bantus in English without having to spend years learning the native language. But in reality no one can believe what he does not understand, even if it is expressed in his own mother tongue. Certainly the Scriptures do not countenance faith in what is unintelligible. Speaking in foreign tongues, though God understands, does not edify because in the congregation no one understands. The message must be translated into the known language. It is better to speak five intelligible words than ten thousand in an unknown tongue. If the people do not understand, how can they say Amen? The sacred writers constantly emphasize doctrine, knowledge, wisdom, and edification. This argument, though given here in a negative form as an objection to an opposing view, must be taken as a positive element in the constructive conclusion that will eventually follow. Allow the addition of another verse. Matthew 28:20 says, "Teaching them to observe all things whatsoever I command you." Nothing is to be left untaught. A person cannot "observe" a doctrine or obey a command unless he knows it. Faith is strictly limited to knowledge.

Romanism's implicit faith contrasts with Calvin's discussion in the *Institutes*, (III, ii). Ridiculing their doctrine he says, "Is this faith—to understand nothing? . . . Faith consists not in ignorance, but in knowledge. . . . By this knowledge [of Christ's propitiation], I say, not by renouncing our understanding, we obtain an entrance into the kingdom of heaven . . . . the apostle [in Romans 10:10] . . . indicates that is not sufficient for a man implicitly to credit [believe] what he neither understands nor even examines; but he requires an explicit knowledge of God and of Christ" (III, ii, 2, 3).

At this point it is a question whether it is better to continue with Calvin's refutation of implicit faith, and so extend the section on Romanism, or to postpone such material and use it positively in the exposition of Calvin. We shall do the latter and turn here to another Roman Catholic author.

M.C. D'Arcy, S.J. published a book of the title *The Nature of Belief.*[6] After a preliminary chapter, aptly described by one of its sub-heads, *Spiritual Crisis in the West*, Chapter II discusses the possibility of truth.

In view of the irrationalism of contemporary society D'Arcy's first task, therefore, is "to restore confidence in the intellect" (p. 30). He describes the various emotional tensions of the present age that interfere with the populace's ability to think clearly. To correct the present nihilism one must "first . . . show that the mind is not material." To do this D'Arcy depends largely on the argument that material bodies can be quantitatively measured, and that which cannot be quantified or dissected into parts is spirit or thought.

The reader must not suppose that the present writer agrees with everything that D'Arcy says. In contrasting the mind's grasping a thought and the hand's grasping a coin, D'Arcy

---

6. Herder Book Co., 1958; reprinted, Greenwood Press, 1976.

says, "The coin is or is not in my hand—that is a fact and not a truth" (p.32). Obviously it is a truth. Did he not print the proposition on the page? Another point of disagreement is D'Arcy's use of imagery, in which he resembles Cardinal Newman and St. Thomas, though he does not seem so extreme as they.

When one author constantly criticizes other authors, the reader may be repelled by the negativism. Let it be repeated that contrasting views bring both sides into sharper focus. And not only so, the writer criticized may set forth some very acceptable material. In these pages D'Arcy makes some excellent points on the distinction between soul and body to the discomfiture of behaviorists. However behaviorism is not the present subject.[7]

After Chapter II has defended *The Possibility of Truth*, Chapter III directly attacks the problem of *Belief*. He begins by distinguishing belief from knowledge. His argument is very plausible. "Belief . . . carries us beyond the obvious in experience and the self-evident in propositions. . . . There is very little that we can know with the certainty of absolute proof. . . . All that falls short of demonstrable certainty has been included under the word 'belief' " (pp. 50-51). Nevertheless "we must be careful not to underrate this belief and reckon it necessarily uncertain. . . . This form [of belief] goes also by the name of faith, and on analysis seems to mean a state of mind . . . of absolute certainty" (p. 52).

The notion of certainty—a notion many other religious writers adopt—requires some scrutiny. People are certain of all sorts of things. Roman Catholics of earlier centuries were certain about the Donation of Constantine; and Neo-Platonic

---

7. Compare Clark, *Behaviorism and Christianity* (Jefferson, Maryland: The Trinity Foundation, 1982).

mysticism infiltrated the church because all the churchmen were certain that Paul's Athenian convert, Dionysius the Areopagite, was the author of the *Divine Names*. His mysticism or negative theology still afflicts, in a variety of modified forms, a number of professing Christians even though they have never heard of the pagan Proclus whom Dionysius plagiarized. In lesser matters some people have been certain that a witch's brew could cure warts, and in government affairs the communists are certain that they shall rule the world. It would seem therefore that certainty has little to do with truth. If so, its insertion in theology and apologetics only renders uncertain the nature and value of faith.

As was said above, D'Arcy moderates some of Newman's extreme positions. It is not essential here to decide rigorously to what extent this is so, for the aim at the moment is more or less confined to presenting various views, even if negatively, as helpful suggestive material. We note therefore that D'Arcy quotes Newman as follows: "There are three conditions of certitude: that it follows on investigation and proof, that it is accompanied by a specific sense of intellectual satisfaction and relief, and that it is irreversible. If the assent is made without rational grounds, it is a rash judgment, a fancy, or a prejudice; if without the sense of finality, it is scarcely more than an inference; if without permanence, it is a mere conviction" (p. 92).

Newman's conditions here certainly rule out the certainty that a witch's brew will cure warts. But do they leave anything untouched? Does "a specific sense of intellectual satisfaction" guarantee that a belief is based on truly rational grounds? Are not irrational grounds sometimes accepted as rational? If the assent is "without permanence," it is "a mere conviction." In that case, how can one distinguish between *certitude* and *conviction*? What justifies the assertion that 'I shall never change my mind as long as I live"? Who knows what he will believe ten years from now? Newman gets rid of warts rather well, but he also removes certainty at the same time.

Although D'Arcy realizes that Newman used some vague and doubtful terms, such as *instinct, sense, illative sense, probable*, he himself, in trying to avoid Newman's infelicities and to present a better version of the general theory (p. 103), introduces terminology equally vague. He asserts in opposition to Newman that "notions can be absolutely valid, that first principles are not assumptions or instincts, and that therefore conclusions can be unconditional" (p. 104). Suggesting timidly that *assent* is not distinct from *conclusion*, he allows that many arguments or conclusions "in which we can find no flaw leave us quite cold, while others touch us to the quick." No doubt this is so, for no one is enthusiastically interested in every possible subject of debate. But if one understands an argument on an uninteresting subject, is not his assent, refrigerated as it may be, as much an assent as his passionate belief that Rubens is better than Rembrandt or that the New York Yankees are superior to the Philadelphia Phillies? Applying his principle to belief in God D'Arcy continues, "Many listen to arguments for the existence of God, and, if unprejudiced, assent, but remain indifferent until some day, please God, they realize the value of God and the call to act on what they know to be true" (p. 105). Here is a major flaw in D'Arcy's argument. He speaks as if we assent to God and are later moved to act on that assent. But this is a mistaken analysis, for in the situation described there are two assents, not just one. First, the man believes that God exists. This may mean that he believes there is some sort of power in the universe superior to man. It might even mean there is power that can be utilized, avoided, or ignored. Belief in God covers a multitude of sins. With three or four billion human beings inhabiting the earth, belief in God usually does not mean belief in the Triune God. In fact "belief in God" hardly means anything. Then later, please the God and Father of our Lord Jesus Christ, the man believes something quite different. The nature of assent in the two cases is the same, but the propositions assented to are altogether different. One can never believe $x$ ; one must believe that x is y.

Beyond this D'Arcy uses some terms as vague as Newman's: "comparative apprehension," "degrees of closeness and obscurity" (based on what I believe to be a misinterpretation of Descartes), "self-evidence," "direct apprehension of reality," "intuition," "dogmatic" as opposed to some other type of assent. In these pages (103-111) there is much that is interesting and much that is suggestive—at least it suggests many problems—but an acceptable view of assent or belief seems to be absent.

If the unphilosophical reader finds a recital of D'Arcy's details somewhat boring, the present writer sympathizes with him. In chapters VI and X there are epistemological and metaphysical analyses, in great detail, but which seem, to one who disagrees with the underlying assumptions, seriously mistaken. What D'Arcy takes as self-evident, another looks on as impossible. Let us therefore skip over to the final chapter on *Divine Faith,* even if we have missed much of the preparatory material.

He briefly sums up this preliminary epistemological material (with which I thoroughly disagree) in a paragraph of rather pleasing literary merit. "We are constantly engaged," he says, "on interpreting natural objects, friends, the world of politics and art and history, and we carry this habit of mind to greater problems, to an interpretation in fact of the whole of reality. Only here we find that the task is too much for us. . . . We are encouraged to find, nevertheless, that knowledge is a trustworthy guide [which allows us to see a] direction and pattern in the universe. To return to an old example, the interpretation of the work of a master in music or painting comes out right and unmistakable when we have assimilated his mind and made it our own by affectionate understanding."

Why cannot we very well understand the mind and art of Felicien Rops with disgust and enmity instead of with affection?

"Is it not then possible that there may be an interpretation of the whole of experience, strange and foolish to those who enjoy their prejudices, but to the ones initiated, the wisdom and power of God? . . . The credentials are there for all to examine, proofs are offered . . . Faith is not vision . . . it is rather the beginning of a new life . . ." (p. 209). On the next page he defines faith as "the act as that whereby we believe without doubting whatever God has revealed. . . . Faith is belief on the authority of God revealing. The motive of faith is the truthfulness of God who speaks. Faith is an act of submission of the intellect to God . . . and at the same time it is a laying hold of some truth which He has revealed."

Divest this of the epistemological basis on which D'Arcy supports it and the statement is very good, with one exception. D'Arcy here makes a distinction between an act of submission to God and something else that happens "at the same time," namely, "a laying hold of" or belief in and acceptance of some true propositions. What is the distinction? Why are not these two the same thing?

Perhaps on the next two or three pages (211-213) D'Arcy inadvertently tends to identify them, thus evincing some confusion; but of this the advanced student must judge for himself by reading the book. One of his sentences is, "Faith therefore is seen so far to consist in the believing of truths on the authority of God" (p. 212).

Yet there is confusion or vagueness, for he continues on the same page to say, "The life of a fox terrier is higher than

that of a foxglove, and the life of a man is in turn above that of a
dog. Let us suppose that a dog were for several hours of the day
allowed to live the life of a human; it would then be exerting
powers which were above the capacity of its nature." So it is
with supernatural faith.

Other authors have pictured man as a bird, for whose
instruction God must descend and chirp. The chirping is not
divine language—birds cannot understand language—it is
human language which God must use for His birds; but unfortunately the divine message cannot be put into bird language,
and God finds it impossible to get His ideas across. This
illustration of the inadequacy of human language is more
extreme than D'Arcy's view, but both, in my opinion, misunderstand that man is the image of God (I Corinthians 11:7).
Since man is God's image, man's language is God's language,
and we think God's thoughts after Him—not some different
analogical thoughts, but God's thoughts themselves. However,
though we reject the Thomistic doctrine of analogical knowledge, Thomas' statement that "Faith is an act of the intellect,
under the command or direction of the will" (p. 213) is excellent, if it is detached from Thomistic empiricism and incorporated into an Augustinian philosophy. Unfortunately some
Reformed theologians, if indeed they wish to do so, are not
completely successful.[8]

## 5. Biblical Data

Although a Christian does not ask for any extended
argument defending the appropriateness of using scriptural
data, he might be encouraged by the fact that the secular
investigations of belief are so various and inconclusive,

8. See my *Language and Theology* (Jefferson, Maryland: The Trinity Foundation,
1980).

depending as they do on experience, that even the secular writers themselves ought to welcome divine revelation. God created man and therefore knows more about human nature than any psychologist could ever discover experimentally. Then, too, the Romanist writers, even though they believe that the Bible is infallible, use it insufficiently and often misinterpret it by reason of tradition, papal pronouncements, and what may be called fallacious scholastic arguments. The Reformers, on the other hand, not only appealed to Scripture, as opposed to the secularists, but to *Sola Scriptura*, as opposed to the Romanists.

For this reason it is appropriate at this point to insert a preliminary amount of scriptural data. Later the discussion of each theologian in turn will also be studded with biblical citations; but a sample here will serve as an acceptable foundation.

Seminaries have traditionally divided theology into two courses. The more elementary one is called Biblical Theology, the more advanced is called Systematic Theology. The first collects all the biblical data, usually in the order of its temporal disclosure to man: Genesis, then Malachi, then the Gospels and Apocalypse. After this fund of information is laid on the table, the theologian reorganizes it systematically. That is, he first collects all the information on God's nature, then all the information on God's rule over the universe, then sin, redemption, and so on. The result is a logical system. This procedure is here followed within a narrower range. First the biblical data will be collected, perhaps not exhaustively, nor altogether in strict historical order, but a sample of what is meant will be given. Then some systematic and general inferences will be attempted.

First, then, the references. God told Noah that there would be a great flood. Genesis 6 may not use the word *faith*, but it makes clear that Noah believed what God said. Abraham is sometimes called the father of the faithful. Not only does the Old Testament describe how firmly he believed God's prophecies, but Galatians in the New Testament identifies Christian faith with the faith of Abraham. Romans 4, Hebrews 11, and James 2, also make Abraham's faith a part of their argument.

The role of faith in the Old Testament should not be minimized. One could use Jacob, Joseph, Moses, Gideon, David, and Daniel (to name only a few) as examples. Sometimes disbelief, the absence of faith, is mentioned; and in Psalm 78:21-22, 32, in addition to the merely historical event, the consequences of unbelief are stated: "Anger also came up against Israel because they believed not in God. . . . For all this they sinned still and believed not in spite of his wondrous works."

The word *believe* in this quotation is a Hebrew term only twice translated *faith*, sometimes translated *truth* or *truly*, but frequently translated *believe*.

One can learn about the fact of faith, i.e., the instances, the nature of faith, its importance and its various relations from negative as well as from positive examples. Isaiah 7:9 says, "If ye will not believe, truly ye shall not be established." This is not now the place to consider whether the KJ translation *will* means that belief is voluntary assent; here we are merely collecting examples of data. II Chronicles 20:20 states the converse: "Believe in the Lord your God, so shall ye be established; believe his prophets, so shall ye prosper."

Since this is not a text book on Old Testament Biblical Theology—Oehler-Day produced a volume of 593 pages—the verses picked must be taken as simply samples. The theme of Biblical Data is even more difficult when we come to the New Testament. A short list must suffice. A verse often quoted is

Hebrews 11:1 Faith is the substance of things hoped for, the evidence of things not seen.

Some people take this as a definition of faith. It is no more a definition than "A triangle is something one studies in geometry courses." It is not even so clear. Most people know what a geometry course is—though with the serious deterioration of public education in the United States fewer people have a satisfactory notion—but hardly anybody knows what the word *substance* means. Is it a substance in the sense that wheat is the substance out of which bread is made? The NAS tries to clarify the verse by translating it

Hebrew 11:1 Faith is the assurance of things hoped for, the conviction of things not seen.

Arndt and Gingrich's Lexicon gives both meanings for *hypostasis: substance* and *conviction*. It also gives *reality* and *actual being*. The more complete Liddell and Scott lists the *act* of *standing under, sediment, abcess, soup, duration, origin, courage, resolution, real nature*, as well as *substance, actual existence, wealth,* and *title deed to property*. The other word in the verse, *evidence* or *conviction (elegchos)*, means *proof, reproof, correction* (Arndt and Gingrich) and *disproof, refutation, scrubbing, catalogue, inventory* (Liddell and Scott). This information should warn the reader that although quoting verses is an indispensable prerequisite for formulating Christian doctrine, much more is required.

Nor is the exact meaning of individual Greek words the only difficulty. It is possible to know accurately every word in a sentence without knowing the meaning of the sentence. For example, James 2:20 speaks of a dead faith. James also says that Abraham was justified by works and not by faith alone. How does this fit in with what Paul says? However let us quote a half a dozen verses or so as a small sample of the data necessary to a study of faith.

Mark 11:22 Have faith in God.

John 6:29 This is the work of God, that you believe
in whom he has sent.
Acts 20:21 Repentance toward God and faith in our
Lord Jesus Christ.
Romans 4:19 Not being weak in the faith . . .
Ephesians 2:8 By grace you have been saved through
faith.
Hebrews 12:2 Looking to Jesus, the leader (ruler,
prince) and perfector of the faith . . .
Jude 20 Building up yourselves on your most holy
faith . . .
Revelation 2:13, 19 Thou . . . hast not denied my
faith . . . I know thy faith.
Revelation 13:10 Here is the patience and the faith of
the saints.
Revelation 14:12 They keep the commandments of
                         God and the faith of Jesus.

These arbitrarily selected verses all contain either the
noun *faith* or the verb *believe* from which root the noun gets its
meaning. This is a very small sample because the verb *believe*,
by rough count, occurs 248 times in the New Testament and the
noun *faith* or *belief* occurs 244 times. No doubt the reader will
be glad that not all 492 verses were quoted.

Here is as good a place as any to sound a warning. The
term *faith* has two very distinct meanings. Sometimes it means
the mental activity of believing. Indeed it is this meaning which
is the subject of the present study. In the list just quoted this
meaning occurs in Mark 11:22, John 6:29, and Acts 20:21;
while the second meaning, namely the propositions believed,
occurs in Revelation 2:13, 19 and 14:12. This second meaning
is prominent in the Pastoral epistles. Although many people
confuse the two and slip from one to the other without realizing
what they are doing, this warning should enable an attentive

reader to identify each throughout the present monograph.

Before we leave the sphere of biblical data and proceed to something more systematic, it may be well to discuss a difficult verse in anticipation of further troubles. The end in view, viewed perhaps from afar, is the definition of faith. Examples of difficulties will help us find the definition. Now, James 2:20 is a puzzling passage. He speaks there of a dead faith and describes it as a faith unproductive of good works. Precisely what a man of dead faith actually believes is not too clear. One thing, however, is clear: The word *faith* here cannot mean "personal trust" in the sense that some popular preachers impose on it in distinction to belief. 'Dead trust' would be an unintelligible phrase. Clearly James means a belief of some sort; and the only belief James mentions is the belief in monotheism. Islam therefore would be a dead faith.

There are some other varieties of faith which may be mentioned as this subsection concludes. Matthew 13 apparently refers to what some theologians call "temporary faith." Hodge (III, p. 68) writes, "Nothing is more common than for the Gospel to produce a temporary impression . . . Those impressed, believe." But Hodge does not say precisely what they believe. He hardly acknowledges that the person in the parable who is represented by the stony places believes anything, even though we read "heareth the word and anon with joy receiveth it." This sounds as if the stony man believed some or even all of the gospel. However, the previous verses describe such men as "seeing, see not; and hearing hear not; neither do they understand;" following which Jesus quotes Isaiah. A person can indeed hear words without understanding them, but can he thus believe them, and can he receive them with joy? Clearly there are troubles here that we must ponder.

Other theologians speak of an "historical" faith, by which, strangely, they do not mean only a belief in the truth of histori-

cal events recorded in the Bible, but also in some, many, or
perhaps all the Biblical norms of morality. Possibly the rich
young ruler would exemplify this sort of faith. He certainly
believed that he had kept all the commandments; but unfortunately this was a mistaken belief. How much else of the Old
Testament he believed (Genesis 17?) is not clear.

One further point may be made before the systematic
exposition begins. It has more to do with church history than
exegesis. In the second century a widespread heresy almost
engulfed and destroyed the Church. It was Gnosticism. The
name comes from the word *gnosis*, knowledge. Later theologians have sometimes contrasted faith with knowledge. This is
the wrong contrast, for two reasons. First, II Peter 1:3 says that
everything pertaining to godliness comes to us through knowledge. There are many supporting references. The Pastorals
have several. The second reason is that the knowledge of which
the Gnostics boasted was a theory of cosmology, including
highly imaginative accounts of what happened before Genesis
1:1.

Admittedly, the Gnostics were devoid of Christian faith;
but the contrast is not between faith and knowledge—it is a
contrast between the different objects known or believed. The
Gnostics knew, or believed in, thirty eons, a docetic incarnation, and a pseudo-atonement. The Christians believed a different set of propositions. Since, however, some students of
evangelistic zeal may question the value of a "merely secular,
psychological" analysis of belief, it is best to show the importance and necessity of saving faith. Then as saving faith is
recognized as a species of generic faith, the analysis will have its
proper setting.

The reader will doubtless be disappointed at the inadequacy and inconclusiveness of the previous paragraphs. But in
a sense that was their purpose: they gave a sample of the

biblical data and by indicating a few of the problems showed the need of a more systematic procedure. One might think that a systematic exposition of faith would now begin with a definition of faith. This would indeed be proper; but the reader would immediately ask, "How do you get that definition from the Bible?" This is what we shall attempt to show, and we shall begin with a survey of Reformation views.

# 6. John Calvin

The section on *Roman Catholic Views* contained some of Calvin's attack on the doctrine of implicit faith. A continuation of this subject will show that arguments which some people dislike as negative—it is unpopular to be negative—are logically as positive and as constructive as any others. To *assert* that some books are *not* interesting is to *deny* that all books *are* interesting. Denials and assertions, positives and negatives, are inseparable. When Calvin *attacks* implicit faith, he *proclaims* the Protestant doctrine of explicit faith. Therefore, we shall continue to quote some lines from the *Institutes*. One must realize, of course, that Calvin is discussing saving faith, for which reason not everything he says is true of generic faith. This is rather obvious and need cause no confusion, for the differences between Islamic, Jewish, or communistic faith and Christian faith can hardly escape notice.

Now, Calvin: "Paul connects faith as an inseparable concomitant with doctrine, where he says . . . 'as the truth is in Jesus . . . [and] the words of faith and good doctrine' . . . . Faith has a perpetual relation to the word. . . . 'These are written, that ye might believe.' . . . . Take away the word, and then there will be no faith left . . . We must further inquire what part of the word it is, with which [saving] faith is particularly concerned. . . . When our conscience beholds nothing but indignation and vengeance, how shall it not tremble with fear? . . . But faith ought to seek God, not fly from him. But suppose we substitute benevolence and mercy. [And Calvin quotes a number of verses] . . . Now we shall have a complete definition of faith, if we say, that it is a steady and certain knowledge of the Divine benevolence towards us, which, being founded on the truth of the gratuitous promise in Christ, is both revealed to our minds, and confirmed to our hearts, by the Holy Spirit" (III, ii, 2, 3, 6, 7).

This emphasis on doctrine, the truth, the word, the promise, sets the standard for Reformation theology. With due respect to Calvin, however, one may ask whether or not the concluding definition tends to confuse faith with assurance. More on this later. It may also be doubted whether the definition is "complete." At least there is more to be said. It is clear, however, that Calvin emphasizes knowledge, in particular the knowledge of God's promise. Hence the object of belief is a proposition.

In reading Calvin one must consider the date of the *Institutes*. This work was first published in 1536. The final edition, much enlarged, came in 1559. The Council of Trent was called in 1542; it recessed in 1547 and resumed in 1551. It recessed again from 1552 to 1562; and its final decisions were confirmed by the Pope in 1564. Thus, Calvin began writing before the Council convened; he finished his work before the Council concluded; and hence his description of Romanism could not be accurately based on the Council's conclusions. He had to use concrete examples from actual authors and preachers. The result is that some of his descriptions of Romanism are not true of what later became the official Roman position.

For example, in III, ii, 8, he says, "They maintain faith to be a mere assent, with which every despiser of God may receive as true whatever is contained in the Scripture." Now, maybe some brash Schoolman or stupid monk said this; but it is not the post-tridentine official position. In the twentieth century Catholic Encyclopedia, faith is stated to be "fiducial assent." Nor is it clear that a despiser of God can receive as true whatever—some things no doubt, but everything?—is contained in the Scripture.

However much we oppose the Roman church, even to asserting the Reformation view that the Papacy is the antichrist, it is unnecessary, and we do our cause no good, to misrepresent these idolators. Hence, since it was impossible to include everything about Catholicism and exclude everything about Calvin in the earlier section, so too in this section they are again intermingled. As a matter of history, therefore, a few paragraphs on the decrees of Trent follow. These decrees contain much that is wrong. They teach that baptism is the instrumental cause of justification and that in justification God makes us just. They assert human cooperation and deny irresistible grace; and many other things, including of course the abominations of the Mass. However, and nonetheless, there are some remnants of Christianity. The quotation following concerns faith, and though mixed with stultifying error, there are some good phrases.

Sixth Session, chapter VIII: "We are therefore said to be justified by faith because faith is the beginning of human salvation. . . . without which it is impossible to please God. . . . We are therefore said to be justified *freely* because none of those things which precede justification—whether faith or works—merit the grace itself of justification . . . otherwise grace is no more grace."

Then follow (Chapter IX) a repudiation of Reformation heretics, (Chapter X), the increase of justification, then on keeping the Commandments, presumption and predestination, perseverance, (Chapters XI, XII, XIII) etc.

After Chapter XVI come some Canons opposing the Reformation view of Justification. For example, "If any one saith that men are justified either by the sole imputation of the justice of Christ. . . . to the exclusion of [infused] grace and the charity that is poured forth in their hearts by the Holy Ghost, and is inherent in them. . . . let him be anathema" (Canon XI).

Even here this is not so bad as it sounds to post-reformation ears; or at least the error is often incorrectly identi-fied. The Romanists included in their term *justification* what the Reformers and the Bible call *sanctification*. This latter of course requires infused grace and love. A more accurate identi-fication of the Romish error would be their complete blindness to biblical justification. They used the term, but they omitted and denied God's judicial, justifying acquittal.

In addition to the decrees of Trent, something from the *Dogmatic Decrees of the Vatican Council* (A.D. 1870) forms an interesting historical note. "Chapter III, *On Faith*. Man being wholly dependent upon God, as upon his Creator and Lord . . . we are bound to yield to God, by faith in his revela-tion, the full obedience of our intelligence and will. And the Catholic Church teaches that this faith, which is a supernatural virtue, whereby, inspired and assisted by the grace of God, we believe that the things which he has revealed are true . . . because of the authority of God himself . . . But though the assent of faith is by no means a blind action of the mind, still no man can assent to the Gospel teaching, as is necessary to obtain salvation, without the illumination and inspiration of the Holy Spirit who gives to all men sweetness in assenting to and believing in the truth. Wherefore faith itself, even when it does not work by charity, is in itself a gift of God, and the act of faith is a work appertaining to salvation, by which man yields volun-tary obedience to God himself, by assenting to and cooperating with his grace, which he is able to resist."

This is certainly not Reformation theology, and some of its phrases clearly contradict the teaching of Scripture. Nevertheless it may appear that Calvin did not correctly anticipate the Tridentine Symbol when he gave the Romish definition of faith as "a mere assent with which every despiser of God may receive as true whatever is contained in the Scripture."

In addition to the fact that Calvin wrote before the Council of Trent assembled, and finished writing before it concluded, misunderstandings, especially on our part today, can arise because of changes in the meanings of words over four centuries. Calvin says "the assent which we give to the Divine word . . . is from the heart rather than the head, and from the affections rather than the understanding." Since the Scripture never contrasts the head and the heart, but frequently contrasts the heart and the lips, one ought to suppose that by *head* Calvin meant the *understanding* and by *heart* the *will*. Nor is "the obedience of faith," which he quotes in the very next sentence, an "affection:" it is a volition. Obedience is always voluntary. A few lines below Calvin speaks more clearly: "It is an absurdity to say, that faith is formed by the addition of a pious affection to the assent of the mind, whereas even this assent consists in a pious affection, and is so described in the Scriptures" (III,ii,8).

If much that Calvin says exposes the errors of Rome, these last words should warn evangelicals not to belittle assent, "mere" assent of the mind, for this voluntary acceptance of the truth is itself a pious action (if not an "affection").

The Larger Catechism (Question 72) will serve as a conclusion for this contrast between Romanism and Calvinism.

"Justifying faith is a saving grace, wrought in the heart of a sinner, by the Spirit and word of God, whereby he, being convinced of his sin and misery, and of the disability in himself and all other creatures to recover him out of his lost condition, not only assenteth to the truth of the promise of the gospel, but receiveth and resteth upon Christ and his righteousness therein held forth, for pardon of sin, and for accepting and accounting of his person righteous in the sight of God unto salvation."

Unfortunately there is one phrase in this answer that seems to deviate from Calvin, and for which the proof text follows an inaccuracy in the King James translation. The phrase is "not only assenteth . . . but receiveth and resteth." The addition of these words seems to be a denial that the assent itself can be "pious." Not to extend this subsection unduly, for some of the later discussion will cover the point, one may study the exegesis of Ephesians 1:13, in Hodge and other commentators. Though it differs somewhat from Hodge, the student may consider this translation: "In whom also you received an inheritance, having heard the word of truth, i.e., the gospel of your salvation, in which [neuter] also having believed, you were sealed . . . ." The emphasis here is on having believed the good news.

The relation between faith and knowledge had been a matter of discussion long before Calvin. Not to mention Clement's *Stromata* (V, 1) or Cyril of Jerusalem (*Catechetical Lectures*, V, 4), we note that Augustine took as a sort of motto *"Credo ut intelligam,"* and Aquinas held that *"Intelligo ut credam."* But the seeming sharpness of the disagreement is modified by the consideration that the two theologians did not use *intelligo* in the same sense. The empirical Aristotelianism of Thomas and the rational Platonism of Augustine separate before questions of faith can be considered. Calvin in general follows Augustine, and his view of Scripture differs from that of Aquinas.

It is true that Calvin seems to place some reliance on the cosmological argument, compromising *Sola Scriptura*; and he also seems to prove or at least to support the truth of Scripture by evidential reasons in the *Institutes* I, viii, whose title is "Rational Proofs to Establish the Belief of the Scripture." A better title would have been, Historical Evidences of the Bible's Divinity. Indeed, the Westminster Confession (I, v) correctly evaluates these evidences and accurately reproduces Calvin's view that the Scriptures are self-authenticating. In fact, in his preceding chapter (I, vii, 5) Calvin so declares. He says explicitly that the Scriptures "ought not to be made the subject of demonstration and argument from reason." Therefore he should not have used the misleading title of I, viii. We ought to understand likewise the intended force of his so-called cosmological arguments, though admittedly they are more embarrassing than chapter eight.

In recent years some disciples of Kierkegaard, and many sincere, though inadequately educated, apologetes, have misinterpreted Calvin's view, and especially some of his still medieval terminology. Perhaps "Thomistic terminology" would be a better expression, for though medieval it remains in common use today. The misapprehension is that when Calvin rejects "reason," and belabors secularists as proud and high minded, and warns against "curiosity," he means to reject logic. This is a rather strange misapprehension, for Calvin is widely castigated as being all too logical. The word *reason* therefore should be understood to mean sensory experience, on which, according to Aquinas, all knowledge is based. The contrast is not between reason and revelation, as if revelation were irrational, but between ordinary human experience with its implications and, on the other hand, divinely revealed information. As for logic we appeal a second time to the "good and necessary consequence" of the Westminster Confession. Those authors who speak of Calvin's "abdication of reason from its sovereignty" either misunderstand or use language almost certainly to be misunderstood in the twentieth century.

Consider this passage which concludes a well written page: "No man can have the least knowledge of true and sound doctrine without having been a disciple of the Scripture. Hence originates all true wisdom. . . . For obedience is the source, not only of an absolutely perfect and complete faith, but of all right knowledge of God" (*Institutes,* I, vi, 2). The following section details the aberrations of a mind that depends on natural resources. This explains Calvin's antagonism toward "curiosity," as mentioned just above—an antagonism that secular thinkers identify as Calvin's original sin. But though he could not include the necessary context in every instance, it is clear enough in some: ". . . observe one rule of morality and sobriety; which is, not to speak, or think, or even desire to know, concerning obscure subjects, anything beyond the information given in the Divine word" (I, xiv, 4).[9] This advice may indeed put astronomy and botany beyond our interest, but in view of Calvin's enormously extensive commentaries, he opened up spacious vistas for "curiosity." There is a great scope for faith and knowledge.

In this scriptural context, not in the context of Aristotelian empiricism, we can formulate a proper view of faith and its relation to knowledge, volition, or anything else pertinent. With our basis in Scripture we need not accept the Thomistic position that we cannot know what we believe and cannot believe what we know.

T.H. Parker is the author of a very fine study on *Calvin's Doctrine of the Knowledge of God* (Eerdmans, revised ed. 1959). If Warfield's *Calvin and Calvinism* (Oxford University Press, 1931) is a must, Parker's book is so likewise. But both these authors flounder on occasion. No doubt the present

---

9. The system of apologetics, defended by the present writer in his other publications, has been vigorously condemned for adhering to Calvin's admonition.

writer does so too: each reader must judge for himself where. But with whatever confusion he may be tainted, Parker's is one he wishes to avoid.

Parker writes (p. 106): "The knowledge of God cannot be regarded as one of the branches of epistemology, but differs fundamentally from all other forms of knowing. . . . Not only is the object of this knowledge different from other objects of his [man's] knowledge, but because the object of this knowledge is God, whose difference from man is such that there exists a religious discontinuity between man and Him, the knowing itself is not of the same kind as those acts of knowing which have for their object something in the same dimension as man. . . . Knowing God is a unique activity in man's experience, having its own categories. It runs the risk, if it borrows from the categories of general epistemology, of destroying itself by turning its direction from its true object, God, to an idol fabricated by itself."

After carefully reading this paragraph one must conclude that the confusion is substantial and not merely verbal. Note that Parker assigns to the knowledge of God categories that are different from those of general epistemology. God is not merely a different object of knowledge: our activity of knowing is epistemologically different. Now, Parker does not enumerate the categories through which other objects are known. Worse, he does not enumerate the categories through which God is known. If he cannot state these two lists of categories, how can he discover that they differ? Of course, if Kantian space and time were categories, which they are not, they would not be applicable to God. But if unity, plurality (trinity), reciprocity, and others are categories, and if these are not applicable to God, how can we assert of God the clearly expressed scriptural descriptions? If the forms of logic are, or are dependent on, the categories, and if they are excluded from the knowledge of God, then we must conclude that God can be both omnipotent and limited, both omniscient and ignorant, both spiritual and corporeal. Why is it permissible to say that a cat is not a dog, yet impermissible to say that God is not Satan? When man's knowing straddles two mutually exclusive epistemologies, he must be beside himself.

If one is less than enthusiastic about this criticism through a distaste for Kant, the objection can be restated in Aristotelian terms. His categories included substance, quality, relation: Athanasius thought that the category of *substance* was necessary; surely the three Persons have *relations* to one another, and to us as well; and is Parker willing to assert that God has no *qualities*? Mercy, for instance? Surely if a theologian wants to maintain that the human mind uses other categories when thinking about God, he ought to name them. To refuse to name them is impolite. To be unable to name them is disastrous.

In spite of some appearances to the contrary Calvin really restricts knowledge to the Scriptures, and so avoids Parker's irrationalism. Calvin says (III, ii, 14) "When we call it knowledge, we intend not such a comprehension as men commonly have of those things which fall under their senses." But in doing so, he is not suggesting different categories, he is not denying the law of contradiction; he is, rather, rejecting Aristotelian empiricism.

In the *Institutes* also (III, ii, 34) he says that "when we are drawn [to Christ] by the Spirit of God . . . we are raised both in mind and in heart above the reach of our own understanding. For illumined by him, the soul receives, as it were, new eyes for the contemplation of heavenly mysteries, by the splendor of which it was before dazzled. And thus the human intellect, irradiated by the light of the Holy Spirit, then begins to relish those things which pertain to the kingdom of God." This language is too figurative for us to pin down its exact meaning, but at least there is no hint in it that the illumination of the Holy Spirit produces an activity apart from the apriori law of contradiction. Indeed Parker inconsistently admits it, for he says, "This must not be taken literally, however; Calvin did not mean that our natural faculties are destroyed when we believe and new faculties given to us by the Spirit" (p. 108). What is given to us is not a new and different set of categories, but *faith*. "It is man who knows, but his knowledge is faith—by virtue of the supernatural gift of God" (p. 109). Calvin in many places denies that the fall made man an irrational being. So far from this is he that his wording sometimes reminds us of the Romanist view that in the fall man lost a *donum superadditum*. Man's "soundness of mind and rectitude of heart were destroyed. . . . Reason by which man distinguishes between good and evil, by which he understands and judges [in matters of mathematics and cosmology], being a natural talent, could not be totally destroyed. . . . In this sense John says, 'the light' still 'shineth in darkness' " (II, ii, 12). Calvin with his consuming interest in saving faith does not write at length on general epistemology; but it is fair, I believe, to say that for him man frequently fails to use the laws of logic properly. Not only are the laws themselves untouched by sin, but also man's obligation to use them is in no sense diminished. Calvin is no anti-intellectual or irrationalist. His comment on Acts 17:22 says, "The mind of man is His [God's] true image."

One author tries to complicate Calvin's theory by distinguishing between *scientia* and *cognitio*. In his Commentary on John 10:38 Calvin writes, "Although [John] places faith after *scientia*,[10] as if it were inferior, he does so because he has to do with unbelieving and obstinate men . . . for rebels wish to be

---

10. Of course, to the confusion of American college students, *scientia* does not mean what they mean by *science*.

sure before they believe. And yet our gracious God . . . prepares us for faith by a *notitia* of his works. But the *cognitio* of God . . . comes after faith." This distinction should not be pressed as if it were a formal theoretical difference. Calvin does not uniformly preserve this distinction. And in this passage from John the *notitia* is the sensible cognition of Christ's miracles. Furthermore, Calvin seems to have stumbled when he concludes that a prior *notitia* must be superior to a temporally later faith.

## 7. Thomas Manton

Was it not Aristotle who said that after a great thinker had laid down the main lines of a system, inferior minds could easily work out the details? There is some truth in this, but it does an injustice if the second thinker happens to be a genius too. Even if not a genius, the later thinker merits the credit of explaining the matter more fully and answering questions that readers of lesser intelligence ask. Now, Thomas Manton (1620-1677) was no genius, but he and others of his age are mistreated when liberals haughtily refer to them as the later scholastic exponents of Protestantism.

Thomas Manton, though vulnerable to several criticisms, nevertheless expresses a view that has often been repeated in evangelical productions. His analysis of belief, expounded in his *Commentary on James*, separates it into three parts: *notitia, assensus,* and *fiducia,* or understanding, assent, and trust. Perhaps even theologians who favor this analysis of belief might omit *fiducia* if they confined themselves to belief as such; for in colloquial language a person who believes that Columbus discovered America in 1492 is not taken as an example of trust. Yet, even so, is he not actually an example of *confidence*?

The word *trust* is a peculiar word, as the word *confidence* has just shown. There is further discussion of *trust*.

Quoting James 2:19 Manton remarks that the faith here is a "bare speculation" and cannot possibly save anyone.

That this faith cannot save is very true. It is no more than a belief in monotheism. This the Moslems possess. But however it may be with Moslems, it seems incorrect to call the faith of devils a bare "speculation." This word often is used to refer to some proposition that is so unverifiable as to be more likely false than true. Granted, Manton also calls it a *knowledge*; and this is better, because on this point, if on nothing else, the devils believe the truth.

He continues: " 'Thou believest;' that is, assentest to this truth." Belief therefore is an act of assent to the truth. Yet, Manton adds, believing is the "lowest act of faith."

Is there a higher act of faith? If so, is it higher because it has a more detailed object, i.e., a greater number of propositions? But in this case it would be still an ordinary act of believing. Or is it higher because some psychological element beyond the act of believing is present? What would that element be?

Manton continues with the object of this belief. "There is one God. He instanceth in this proposition, though he doth limit the matter only to this." This is a now rare usage of the verb, not noun, *to instance*. It means, to give an instance; the proposition, "there is one God," is therefore an instance of specification of what the man believes, Manton suggests that the man believes or assents to "other articles of religion." This is doubtless true, for nearly everyone who believes in any sort of God believes something else about him beyond bare existence. That the man has an extensive Jewish or Christian theology, however, is not clear.

"Thou doest well," quotes Manton; "it [the Scriptural

phrase] is an approbation of such assent, so far as it is good and not rested in."

Again Manton has described the act as voluntary assent . . . naturally, all assent must be voluntary. But what also needs to be noted here are the words "rested in." When we say we rest in, or should not rest in, this or that, do we mean that in addition to *notitia* and *assensus* there is some other psychological element in saving faith called "resting " ? Or does it mean that saving faith, rather than being psychologically different, must be an assent to other propositions in addition to monotheism? The latter seems to be the case, whether or not Manton meant it so. We should not "rest in," i.e., be satisfied with the single proposition, ("There is but one God.") This proposition even the devils accept. But for salvation men must not only accept the monotheistic proposition, but as well other propositions relating to the Atonement.

On the next page Manton notes that the devils assent to this one truth and to other truths revealed in the word, even to "many truths in the Scriptures" (on the following page). But how much of the Bible the devils believe, justification by faith perhaps, is a question that we in our ignorance of satanic psychology cannot answer. Manton apparently wants to maximize the devils' orthodoxy.

"Bare assent," says Manton, "to the articles of religion doth not infer true faith. True faith uniteth to Christ, it is conversant about his person." Two factors seem to be confused in Manton's mind: the psychology and the propositions. Does this quotation mean that saving faith, in addition to belief in monotheism, must also include the Chalcedonian Christology? Certainly an assent to Chalcedon, however "bare," is "conversant about his person." Or does Manton's statement mean that the devils themselves subscribe to Chalcedon, and that "conversant" is a psychological element in addition to assent? It would seem so because otherwise no contrast could be made between "*assent* to the articles of religion" and "*conversant* about his person."

Faith "is not only *assensus axiomati*, an assent to a Gospel maxim or proposition; you are not justified by that, but by being one with Christ. It was the mistake of the former age to make the promise, rather than the person of Christ, to be the formal object of faith."

The mention of the person of Christ is pious language. Similar expressions are common today. One slogan is, "No creed but Christ." Another expression, with variations from person to person, is, Faith is not belief in a proposition, but trust in a person.[11]

Though this may sound very pious, it is nonetheless destructive of Christianity. Back in the twenties, before the Methodist Church became totally apostate, a liberal in their General Conference opposed theological precision by some phrase centering on Christ, such as, Christ is all we need. A certain pastor, a remnant of the evangelical wing of the church, had the courage to take the floor and ask the pointed question, "Which Christ?"

The name Jesus Christ, at least since 1835 in Strauss' *Leben Jesu*, has been applied to several alleged persons. Strauss initiated the "Life of Jesus Movement." It ran through Ernest Renan to Albert Schweitzer.[12] But the persons de-

---

11. In recent years the neo-orthodox and pseudo-evangelicals have propounded the pious nonsense that the Greek word for faith (*pistis*) should be understood by its use for a Hebrew term and not in its Greek meaning. The Hebrew term or terms mean trust or faithfulness and not belief. James Barr, who can in no sense be thought favorable to what Manton calls "the mistake of the former age" i.e., "the mistake" of the Protestant reformers, in his superbly scholarly volume, *The Semantics of Biblical Language* (Oxford University Press, 1961), reduces the pseudo-evangelical view to unscholarly ruins.

12. Compare Geerhardus Vos, *The Self-Disclosure of Jesus,* George H. Doran, 1926.

scribed are nothing like the person described in the Creed of Chalcedon, nor, for that matter, are they alike amongst themselves. It is necessary therefore to ask, Which Christ? or, Whose Christ? The Christian or Biblical answer is the Creed of Chalcedon. A person can be identified only by a set of propositions.

This is what Manton refers to as the mistake of the former age. Thomas Manton was a Puritan of the seventeenth century, and when he speaks of "the former age," he is not referring to apostate Romanism, but to the Reformers themselves. Hence he is a witness that they defined faith as an assent to the promise of the Gospel. By the same token, he wishes to introduce some other element into faith in addition to this act of will. What is it? He answers, "There is not only *assent* in faith, but *consent*[13]; not only an assent to the truth of the word, but a consent to take Christ. . . . True believing is not an act of the understanding only, but a work of all the heart."

A careful study of these words, and of the complete context in Manton, plus a comparison with the Scripture, should conclude that Manton is confused. The first point is that the word *consent* receives no explanation. It makes a pleasant alliteration with *assent*, but literary style is no substitute for analysis. Is "consent" an act of will? Ordinary language would make it seem so; but if so, how is it different from assent? If "consent" is not voluntary, and if it cannot be an act of the understanding either, what sort of mental state is it? Then too, when he says that "true believing is not an act of the understanding only, but a work of all the heart," he is not accurately confronting "the former age." The former age never said that

---

13. Possibly the first systematic theologian to use this term was John of Damascus or Damascene: "fides est non inquisitus consensus;" i.e., "faith is an unquestioned consent."

true believing, or false believing either, is an act of the under-standing only. The former age and much of the later ages too specify assent in addition to understanding. They make this specification with the deliberate aim of not restricting belief to understanding alone. One can understand and lecture on the philosophy of Spinoza; but this does not mean that the lecturer assents to it. Belief is the act of assenting to something under-stood. But understanding alone is not belief in what is understood.

Manton himself acknowledges, "I confess some expres-sions of Scripture seem to lay much upon assent, as I John 4:2 and 5:1; I Corinthians 12:3; Matthew 16:17; but these places [Manton strangely says] do either show that assents, where they are serious and upon full conviction, come from some special revelation; or else, if they propound them as evidences of grace, we must distinguish times."

Now, Matthew 16:17 is not clearly a special revelation. It can well be, and more probably is, an illumination such as God gives to every believer. Nor is I Corinthians 12:3 a special revelation: it refers to all men—it is a completely general statement—and cannot apply only to the few recipients of special revelation. Unless therefore one wishes to be very dog-matic about Peter in Matthew, all of these verses, in Manton's opinion, are to be set aside, are to be explained away, by "distinguishing the times." True enough, God administered the covenant in the Old Testament in a manner different from his administration of the New. Then too, but the differences are much less important, the apostolic age, and the following two centuries, faced difficulties that do not so directly trouble us now. But such historical differences are entirely irrelevant to the present discussion. Whether the propositions and promises of the Old Testament were more vague and less specific than those in the New, and whether the truths of the Gospel seemed more "contrary to the ordinary and received principles of reason" there than now (which is much to be doubted), all this is irrelevant because the mental act of believing is the same in every age and every place. Manton's account of faith is therefore confused, and it has led him to set aside some instructive New Testament material.

The crux of the difficulty with the popular analysis of faith into *notitia* (understanding), *assensus* (assent), and *fiducia* (trust), is that *fiducia* comes from the same root as *fides* (faith). The Latin *fide* is not a good synonym for the Greek *pisteuo*. Hence this popular analysis reduces to the obviously absurd definition that faith consists of understanding, assent, and faith. Something better than this tautology must be found.

## 8. John Owen

If now Thomas Manton has deserved mention, all the more so does his younger and greater contemporary, John Owen (1616-1683), who, among other things, wrote a four thousand page commentary on Hebrews. Here his smaller four hundred and fifty page book on *Justification by Faith* compels our attention. The page numbers are those of the Sovereign Grace edition of 1959.

On page 70, Owen begins an examination of the nature of faith. But the reader must take care. The examination is introduced thus: "Of the nature of faith in general, of the especial nature of justifying faith, of its *characteristical* distinctions from that which is called faith but is not justifying. . . ."

No objection can be made to such an examination; but the student should take care to understand what the nature of faith is in general. Justifying faith is a species of faith, and if one does not know what faith in general is, one cannot know what the faith is that justifies. Does Owen keep this distinction clear?

Unfortunately, he does not make it sufficiently clear to us. In fact he says, "The distinctions that are usually made concerning faith . . . I shall wholly pretermit; not only as obvious and known, but as not belonging to our present argument." Owen seems to have had an optimistic view of his generation. But even if these distinctions were as obvious and well known then as he says, they are not so today. But even "pretermitting" much, Owen cannot escape giving some indication of what the act of believing is.

His very next paragraph speaks of a non-justifying "historical faith." It is not because this faith has much to do with history that it is called historical. In addition to events of history, this faith believes the promises of the Gospel. "But it is so called from the *nature of the assent* [ital. his.] wherein it doth consist." Apparently then there are two kinds of assent. All faith is assent; but justifying faith is a different variety of assent. What this difference specifically is, Owen does not say. He indeed says the difference does not lie in the object of the faith, the proposition believed, but in the nature, or psychological characteristics of this particular type of assent. We would like to know what this different psychology is.

Owen is quite clear that "all faith is an *assent* upon testimony" (p. 72). "Divine faith is an assent upon a divine testimony." Obviously divine testimony is different from human testimony; and as the great Puritan said, the effects of some beliefs differ vastly from the effects of other beliefs. But differences in effects as well as in objects are irrelevant to the question whether there are species of believing. It is to be feared that some notion of "species of beliefs" has been confused with "species of believing." Nor is a reference to a temporary faith as opposed to a permanent faith any more relevant. In fact Berkhof (*op. cit.* p. 501) who follows Owen, adds that temporary faith may last all through one's life, that it is not necessarily hypocritical, and that it includes a stirring of the conscience. No wonder he remarks that "Great difficulty may be experienced in attempting to distinguish it from saving faith." This view also bears on the doctrine of assurance. Yet Owen says, "Justifying faith is not a higher, or the highest degree of this faith, but is of another kind or nature" (p. 72). Yet all his evidence shows not a different type of believing, but a different object of belief. He refers to: (1) different causes, (2) different objects of a previous or preparatory belief, and (3) different objects of faith (p. 80), though he had previously ruled out objects as the difference.

As Owen's account continues, the confusion grows worse. Not only does he misunderstand the Roman position, describing their faith as an assent that does not produce obedience; but also he is dissatisfied with "such a firm assent as produceth obedience unto all divine commands" (p. 81): dissatisfied because something further is necessary. For Owen, faith seems to have three main characteristics, the third of which has eight subdivisions.

The first of these three is assent to the truth: "all divine faith is in general an assent unto the truth that is proposed unto us upon divine testimony." The second point is rather a reassertion of the first. The only difference seems to be that the first refers to some limited number of truths a given individual happens to know, while the second includes "all divine revelation," or even "all divine truth," a phrase that includes divine truth that God has not revealed. Presumably Owen did not mean what he said. But even with the proper restriction, it is not likely that a new Christian, recently justified, understands and assents to every proposition in the Bible. After a lifetime of study a learned theologian could hardly know so much. But, one may say, even the new Christian assents to Biblical infallibility. Quite so, that is a single proposition. Does he then have *implicit* faith in all the other Biblical propositions? On the contrary, Evangelicalism excludes the Romish doctrine of implicit faith. Hence justification cannot depend on our assent to all revealed truth. Justifying faith must be an assent to some truths, not all. Even Owen himself, after having said "all divine revelation," restricts justifying faith to some truths only. But in addition to whatever, all or some, is believed, Owen insists that justifying faith must include certain *causes* and *adjuncts* beyond assent.

His third paragraph begins with an explicit denial that faith is an assent, "be it never so firm and stedfast, nor whatever effects of obedience it may produce." Nor does it equally respect all divine revelation, but only some. Then follow eight points, mainly negative.

(1) Assent is not "an act of the understanding only." Owen's immediate refutation is hardly pertinent; but since no one ever held the point he opposes, for everyone adds something to simple understanding, one may take Owen's first subpoint merely as an attempt to be complete.

(2) Here Owen objects to the proposition that "All divine truth is equally the object of this assent" (p. 82). If it were, so his refutation goes, the proposition that Judas was a traitor would as much effect our justification as that Christ died for our sins. Near the end of this monograph an attempt will be made to specify what proposition or propositions are essential to saving faith. Owen's adverb *equally* justifies his assertion, though he might have added (if it were his opinion) that the proposition about Judas can be a part of justifying faith.

(3) He next denies that "This assent unto all divine revelation may be true and sincere where there hath been no *previous work* of the law, nor any conviction of sin." Owen may well be correct in making this denial, even though the sudden conversion of Paul seems to conflict with it. But in any case and no

matter how true, the paragraph contributes nothing to an analysis of the act of believing.

(4) Point four is very confused, and point (5) asserts, what is at best doubtful, that the devils in James assent to everything in the Bible. Point (6) asserts that hope and trust are not contained in a "mere" assent to the truth, "but they require other actings of the soul than what are peculiar unto the understanding only." But is not Owen off the track? Of course hope and trust require the volition of assent as well as an understanding of the promise or hope.

Point (7) strays completely away from Scripture and depends entirely on introspective experience. Thus his objection to assent here is given solely on his own authority, rather than upon the authority of Scripture. It should be obvious by now that Owen has neither refuted the position that saving faith is a volitional assent to an intellectual proposition, nor presented any alternative analysis of its nature.

(8) Point 8, however, is indubitable because it is a puerile tautology. "That faith alone is justifying which hath justification actually accompanying it. . . . To suppose a man to have justifying faith and not to be justified, is to suppose a contradiction." Of course it is; but for that very reason it is a fallacy to conclude "Wherefore it is sufficiently evident that there is somewhat more required unto justifying faith than a real assent unto all divine revelations" (p. 83).

Owen continues for several difficult pages. He objects to identifying the object of faith with Christ's promise of forgiveness. Instead he maintains that Christ himself is the object of justifying faith. Although this sounds very pious, Owen and others might not have said this, if instead of the term *faith* they had used the Scriptural word *believe.* When we believe a man, we believe what he says. Nor does it help Owen's view to insist on the scriptural phrase, *believe in Christ,* as something essentially different from believing Christ. As we said before, believing in a man may indicate a willingness to believe what he will say in the future as well as what he has said in the past. But belief must always have a proposition as its proper object, and therefore must be assent. Owen, let it be repeated for the sake of clarity, does not deny that assent must always somehow be included in faith. Speaking of the promises of forgiveness he says, "It cannot be but that in the actings of justifying faith, there is a peculiar assent to them. Howbeit, this being only *an act of the mind,* neither the whole nature nor the whole work of faith can consist therein" (p. 87). Now it may well be said that the work or results of faith are several, but such results, such as the preaching of the gospel by an evangelist, are not justifying faith—they are works of righteousness, none of which justify; but if faith or believing itself is not *an act of the mind,* there remains no hope for finding it anywhere else. Dare we suggest that it is the work of the fingers, lungs, or stomach?

All the foregoing comes from Owen's chapter on the *causes* and *object* of justifying faith; and this may to a certain extent excuse the confusion. The following chapter is the *nature* of justifying faith; and it would seem better to have described what belief is before specifying the object of particular beliefs.

At the beginning he remarks that the faith he is discussing is a sincere faith. So be it. Assent is always sincere. No matter what a person believes, he believes it sincerely. A person does not always sincerely state what he believes. He may obscure or even deny his beliefs. But assent to a proposition is *ipso facto* sincere.

Owen then gives negative as well as positive examples. "The unbelief of the Pharisees . . . is called the 'rejecting of the counsel of God' . . . most of those who rejected the Gospel by their unbelief, did it under the notion, that the *way of salvation* and blessedness proposed therein was not a way answering divine goodness . . ." (p. 94-95). Surely this quotation is a statement of truth; but it confutes much that Owen has said, for whereas the disciples assented to Christ's statements when they understood them, the Pharisees assented to or believed contradictory propositions. Therefore, one must reject what Owen says a few lines below; to wit, "unbelievers . . . may give an assent unto the truth of it [the gospel], so far as it is a mere act of the mind." This is logical nonsense, psychological impossibility, and theological confusion. His only defense here, just a few lines below, is that he is no longer talking about sincere faith but only insincere faith.

However severe this criticism of Owen may seem, let not the student suppose that Owen is to be despised. He is one of the greatest Puritans, and we should be extremely happy if we could make as few mistakes as they did. Furthermore, for all the confusion on this point, Owen nonetheless seems to acknowledge that believing is voluntary assent to an understood proposition. Put aside questions as to the object or objects believed, recognize that phrases not containing the words *voluntary* or *assent* may nonetheless have the same meaning, and realize that the act of belief is psychologically the same no matter what is believed, and it is hard to find a phrase descriptive of belief better than voluntary assent.

Thus in his great commentary on Hebrews, at chapter eleven, verse 3, Owen says, " 'By faith we understand,' that is, by faith we assent unto the divine revelation. . . . we come not only to assent unto it as true, but to have a due comprehension of it [creation] in its cause, so as that we may be said to understand it. . . . Those who firmly assent unto divine revelation, do understand the creation of the world, as to its truth, its season, its manner, and end." Perhaps Owen is too optimistic as to the extent of our understanding; but again faith or belief is a volitional assent to an understood proposition.


## 9. Charles Hodge

Charles Hodge, on all counts, is a theologian whose views must be considered. He is the soul and center of American Presbyterianism, properly so-called. His discussion of faith begins in Vol. III, page 41, of his *Systematic Theology*, with the words, "The first conscious exercise of the renewed soul is faith. . . . In the order of nature [the stages in which salvation advances] it must precede repentance." Though the first of these two sentences shows that Hodge is chiefly interested in saving faith, he must perforce say something about generic faith in order to produce any respectably comprehensive theory. The second sentence is doubtful. When such doubtful, vague, or puzzling statements appear, it is worth the time and trouble to analyze them. In this case the difficulty lies in the colloquial use of these terms. Presumably Hodge means that one must believe the gospel (faith) and by so doing learn that repentance from sin is necessary. But etymologically *repentance* means a change of mind, not necessarily restricted to specifically moral matters. It can include a change of mind with reference to all theology, and that too beyond a simple understanding of the doctrines such as any infidel may easily achieve, so as to take in the belief that those understood doctrines are true. In this sense faith and repentance, both gifts of God, are the same thing. Hodge lacks clarity here because he separates faith from repentance by imposing unacceptable limits on both. Faith includes the moral precepts; and repentance, though not colloquially, surely includes the belief that Jesus is Lord. If they are separated, and if repentance is limited to sin

and morality, it becomes a subdivision of faith; but if repentance has the broad meaning of any change of mind, faith is its
subdivision. What then is the precise nature of faith?

"Faith . . . is assent to the truth" (p. 42). Here and elsewhere in this section Hodge emphasizes *trust* as being the
meaning of the Greek word. Some authors and many preachers
contrast *trust* in a person with *belief* in a proposition. They
often disparage "intellectual belief." They must then disparage
all belief, since there is no other kind. But if trust and belief are
different things, even if not antithetical things, how is trust
defined? When a preacher does not tell his congregation what
he means by his main terms, the people are confused, often
without realizing it. But Hodge does better. He speaks most
frequently of trusting that a statement is true, rather than trust
in a person. In fact, on the same page he adds that faith is "that
state of mind in which a man receives and relies upon a thing as
true." He connects this with trust by saying, "To regard a thing
as true is to regard it as worthy of trust" (p. 43); and so he does
not divorce trust from truth, but continues with a quotation
from St. Augustine, "To believe is nothing else than to think
with assent." Some of his following pages seem inconsistently
to modify this view, but, as we shall see, this is, all in all,
Hodge's basic position.

Speaking more particularly of saving faith, but with
explicit references to generic faith also, Hodge admirably
rejects the flowery rhetoric of those platform theologians who
call "faith a special organ for the eternal and holy. It is not
necessary [says Hodge] to assume a special organ for historical
truths, a special organ for scientific truths, and another for the
general truths of revelation, and still another for the eternal
and holy" (p. 44). Even "Limiting it to a consciousness of
reconciliation with God [as J.E. Erdmann did] is contrary to
the usage of Scripture and of theology" (p. 45). Inadequate also

are those views which try to define faith as intermediate between opinion and knowledge. For example, "Locke defines faith to be the assent of the mind to propositions which are probably but not certainly true. . . . To believe is to admit a thing as true, according to Kant, upon grounds sufficient subjectively, insufficient objectively. . . . In all these cases the only difference between opinion, belief, and knowledge is their relative strength" (pp. 46-47). Presumably Hodge means to reject any view that depends on relative strength, even if opinion and knowledge can be clearly defined.

A puzzling paragraph comes a little later, for on pages 51-52 Hodge describes several psychological variations of faith, concluding that faith is not always a voluntary assent, on the ground that sometimes people believe against their will, and in other instances wish they could believe, but cannot. These two cases supposedly show that belief is not within the power of the will. The argument is of course fallacious, for even if a person strongly dislikes a theory or doctrine, and reluctantly considers it carefully, perhaps with a view to refuting it, the evidence for it may prove overwhelming and with pain and regret he accepts it, against his previous will, but nevertheless voluntarily.

Under the heading "Definitions Founded on the Objects of Faith," there is likewise some confusion. Actually Hodge does not discuss the objects of faith, but reverts to the accompanying circumstances, in particular the distinction between faith and knowledge. If we believe a certain proposition because someone informs us about it, we have faith; but if we prove it for ourselves, we have knowledge. Note that it is the same proposition in both instances. Faith is not distinguished from knowledge by its object, as the subhead promised, but by our method of learning it. "When he understands the demonstration of that proposition, his faith becomes knowledge" (p.

54). A more consistent dependence on the object believed would result in a more consistent solution of the problem. But when Hodge, by making knowledge depend on demonstration, concludes that "faith means belief of things not seen, on the ground of testimony" (p. 62), a curious situation has arisen. Stated in other words, Hodge is saying that we believe the "thing" because we believe the testimony. This reduces to the position that "faith or belief is a belief by means of belief."

A few pages ago Hodge seemed to have rejected the notion that the distinction between faith, opinion, and knowledge was based on their relative "strength." But now the rejection is not so clear. Echoing some Thomistic sentiments he explains that faith is not knowledge because we *believe* what we cannot *prove*. To quote: "Reason begins . . . with taking on trust what it neither comprehends nor proves. . . ." In one sense of the words this is utter nonsense. Reason or no reason, a person cannot take on trust what someone states in an incomprehensible foreign language. Hodge is not guilty of nonsense such as this. He means that we may believe a geometrical theorem without having deduced it ourselves. This is not nonsense: It is tautology. It merely means that we have not demonstrated what we have not demonstrated. His following sentence is, "Faith is a degree of certainty less than knowledge and stronger than probability" (p. 62).

One must ask, By what thermometer are these degrees measured? Are the units centimeters or ounces? One must also ask, What is probability? The probability of shooting twelve with two dice is one over thirty-six. Then further, are there not students who, after demonstrating a theorem, are more certain of some teen-age superstition than of Euclid's reasoning? Much, nearly all, of Hodge's confusion arises from his empirical epistemology. "The ground of knowledge is sense or reason" (p. 75). He thinks that science *proves* the truth of its laws, *demonstrates* them, with the result that the laws of physics are not tentative hypotheses but eternal truths. This was of course the commonly accepted Newtonian position of the nineteenth century; but the twentieth century has almost without exception rejected it. Einstein replaced Newton, and no one yet knows who will replace Einstein in the twenty-first century.[14]

Hodge holds that science depends on "sense and reason;" but if *sense* is unclear, reason is more so. This monograph is far from denying that "Faith is founded on the testimony of God" (p. 64). But the axiom that the Bible *is* the Word of God does not justify Hodge's notion of what he calls knowledge. Whereas Hodge seems to limit reason to the deduction of physical laws from sensory observations, one might better define reason as the deduction of theology from Scripture; or, still better, simply the deduction of conclusions from premises. Antichristian scientists take advantage of Hodge's phraseology, even though few have ever heard of Hodge, and conclude that faith is unreasonable, irrational, and that we all should adopt "scientism" as the true philosophy. On the contrary the present writer holds that it is *rational* to believe what God reveals. Hodge's seeming limitation of reason to physics is unfortunate. Nevertheless, Hodge agrees that "Faith is the reception of *truth* . . . the record which God has given to his Son" (p. 65), and he quotes I John 5:10 in Greek.[15] Hodge adds, "Its [faith's] object is what God has revealed." Then below, on the same page, "Faith is the reception of truth. . . ."

Unfortunately, the confusion as to kinds of faith soon

---

14. Compare *The Philosophy of Science and Belief in God* (Jefferson, Maryland: The Trinity Foundation, 1987); and *Horizons of Science,* ed. Carl F.H. Henry (Harper & Row, 1978), last chapter.

15. Compare my commentary on *First John* (Jefferson, Maryland: The Trinity Foundation, 1980).

reappears (p. 67). Of course Jewish faith is not Islamic faith, nor is either of these Christian faith. One might also list political faith and a faith in A.T.&T. stock. But this is not a difference in the definition of faith: It is a difference in the object or propositions believed. They are still all assents. Many theologians fall into this confusion.

These criticisms do not mean that Hodge's theology is bad. On the contrary, it is very good. Every man makes mistakes, but in theology Hodge makes fewer and those less in importance than any other I have read. The criticism is that he obscures his good theology by setting it in a background of false philosophy, and this obscures the truth and confuses the reader. No doubt he would direct the same criticism against me, for he is very convinced of the Scottish common sense philosophy which I regard as horrible.

However, he is not so irrational as my criticisms may have suggested. He probably had not heard of Kierkegaard, but he answers him clearly and bluntly. "The assumption that reason and faith are incompatible; that we must become irrational in order to become believers is, however it may be intended, the language of infidelity; for faith in the irrational is of necessity itself irrational. It is impossible to believe that to be true which the mind sees as false. This would be to believe and disbelieve the same thing at the same time. . . . Faith is not a blind, irrational conviction. In order to believe, we must know what we believe, and the grounds upon which our faith rests" (p. 83). Here we have a perfectly clear assertion of the universal rule of logic. No one can deny the law of contradiction and defend Christianity. Later on, after one or two confusing sentences, Hodge says explicitly, "The cognition of the import of the proposition to be believed, is essential to faith; and consequently faith is limited by knowledge. We can believe only what we can know, i.e., what we intelligently apprehend" (p. 84).

This is an admirable statement, even though it obviously uses the term *knowledge* in a sense different from that which he previously used. It also becomes clouded over when he wonders "Whether faith is purely an intellectual exercise" (p. 89). If by these words he meant to suggest that faith is a volitional as well as an intellectual activity, there could be no criticism; but when he explicitly mentions "affections," the introduction of an emotional element seems to be intended.[16] That emotions sometimes accompany volitional decisions cannot be denied; but this is far from insisting that an intellectual decision has emotion as a necessary ingredient. In connection with Romanism Hodge says, "Regarding faith as a mere [pejorative language] intellectual or speculative act [though Thomas did not regard faith as a speculative or philosophical act], they consistently deny that it [faith] is necessarily connected with salvation. According to their doctrine a man may have true faith, i.e., the faith which the Scriptures demand, and yet perish" (p. 90). To support this statement Hodge quotes the Council of Trent, Session vi, Canon 28. But the Canon says no such thing. It errs in the opposite direction, or it says that though grace (not as Protestants define it) be lost, faith remains and the person does not perish.

In contrast with Romanism, as Hodge understands it, he says, "Protestants with one voice maintain that the faith which

---

16. Not so in Jonathan Edwards' *A Treatise Concerning Religious Affections.* Toward the end of Part I, Section I, he says, "The *will* and the *affections* of the soul are not two faculties; the affections are not essentially distinct from the will, nor do they differ from the mere *actings* of the will." Similarly Thomas Goodwin (1600-1679) in his *An Exposition of Ephesians,* at Ephesians 1:14 (Sovereign Grace Book Club, 1958, p. 259, bottom paragraph) states as an accepted fact that "You know the soul of man hath two great faculties . . . he hath an understanding, he hath a will and affections." Since the soul is said to have two functions, it is clear that affection and volition are synonymous.

is connected with salvation is not a mere intellectual exercise" (p. 90). And he quotes Calvin, "fidei sedem non in cerebo esse, sed in corde" (Commentary on Romans 10:10). He also quotes the *Institutes* III, ii, 8, "the heart rather than the brains, and the affections rather than the intelligence." There are two or three difficulties in this section from Calvin. First, *cerebri,* brains, is the language of behaviorism and should never be thus used in the twentieth century. In the sixteenth century, however, it was a metaphorical term for the mind or intellect. Second, and more seriously, the Scriptures make no distinction between the head and the heart, as if mathematics came from the head and faith from the heart. The Old Testament frequently contrasts the heart and the lips—sincerity versus hypocrisy—but the term *heart,* at least seventy-five percent of the time in the Old Testament, means the mind or intellect.

It may seriously deface the organization of this monograph, and it certainly interrupts the account of Charles Hodge, but because of its importance, including the fact that Calvin seems involved too, not to speak of hundreds of present day pastors, it seems essential to include an awkwardly lengthy interlude on the alleged contrast between the head and the heart—an interlude devoted to Biblical exegesis.[17]

The aim of citing the following Biblical data—an unusually extended list for such studies as this, but only a small fraction of the textual instances—is to show as clearly as possible what the term *heart* means. Were the misunderstanding less pervasive, were the pastors less Freudian and more Biblical, were the congregations less confused and misled, a much briefer list would have sufficed. Present ignorance, how-

---

17. Anyone who wishes to write or preach on Biblical psychology must, really must, read *The Bible Doctrine of Man* by John Laidlaw, second edition, T. & T. Clark, Edinburgh, 1895. The present paragraphs use, add to, and subtract from Laidlaw's superb study.

ever, would justify even a more extensive documentation than that which now follows.

Genesis 6:5 The Lord saw . . . that every intent of the thoughts of his heart was only evil continually.

Here the *heart* is connected with thinking. Whatever emotions the sons of God may have had upon seeing the daughters of men, the verse refers to their thoughts—and not merely thoughts with regard to ungodly marriages, but with reference to their conduct in general. Their thoughts surely included thoughts on finances and most certainly thoughts on theology. They thought it useless to think of God.

Genesis 8:21 The intent [King James: imaginations] of man's heart is evil from his youth.

This verse, like the preceding, indicates theological thinking. The activity of intellection is clear. A second activity is also implied in both these verses: the word *intent* in the phrase "the intent of the heart" seems to indicate volition. The Hebrew word means both *concept* and *purpose.* Very obviously this is not emotional, for the verse pictures a settled, lifelong philosophy. Emotions are sudden, transient upheavals. Since men's conduct is governed by these lifelong principles, the term *heart* also indicates volition as well as intellection.

Genesis 17:17 Abraham fell on his face and laughed and said in his heart, Will a child be born to a man one hundred years old?

Perhaps Abraham felt some emotion of contempt at God's stupidity, but his *heart* raised an intellectual objection to God's promise. He said, because he thought in his heart, that a man of a hundred cannot engender nor can a woman of ninety give birth to a child. This is biological intellection; and it is sound thinking, except when God miraculously intervenes.

Genesis 20:6 Yes, I know that in the integrity of your heart you have done this.

No doubt Abimilech experienced sexual emotions upon seeing beautiful Sarah, but in this verse and in the preceding the *heart* is described as thinking that Sarah was Abraham's sister and not his wife. This was an intellectual judgment, and it is the judgment, not the emotion, that is assigned to the heart.

Exodus 4:21 I will harden his heart so that he will not let the people go.

Here the intellectual judgment is in the background. Of course Pharaoh had judged or thought that the Israelite slaves were financially valuable to Egypt; but the point of this verse has to do with volition rather than with intellection. God would harden or strengthen Pharaoh's will to refuse Moses' demand. Perhaps fifteen or twenty percent of the Old Testament instances of the term *heart* refer to volition rather than to intellection. Naturally, as we shall see, volition always depends on a prior intellection. Very few instances of the term *heart* refer distinctly to emotions.

Exodus 7:3 says the same thing.

Exodus 35:5 Whoever is of a willing heart, let him bring . . . [a] contribution: gold, silver, bronze.

The Hebrew term for *willing* can be translated *voluntary* or *magnanimous*. The term *heart* therefore stands for volition and not emotion.

Deuteronomy 4:9 Keep thy soul diligently, lest thou forget the things which thine eyes have seen, and lest they [the things] depart from thy heart all the days of thy life.

Here the heart is described as the repository of historical information, which information includes the Ten Commandments and the subsidiary laws. No doubt Moses here commands voluntary obedience, but the contents of the heart are propositions concerning historical events. The heart *knows.* There is nothing emotional here.

I Samuel 2:1 My heart exults in the Lord.

It is true that sometimes the term *heart* refers to emotions. Here, rather clearly, Hannah is emotional. Of course she is also theological, especially if we hold that she prefigures the Virgin Mary's *Magnificat.* Nevertheless, Hannah and Mary both spoke emotionally. In about ten percent of the Old Testament instances of the word *heart* emotions are definitely indicated.

I Samuel 2:35 I will raise up for myself a faithful priest who will do according to what is in my heart and in my soul [King James: mind].

The terms *heart* and *soul* here are presumably synonyms, as in the New Testament "heart, soul, strength and mind" are synonyms for the purpose of inclusiveness. Here *soul* (Hebrew *nephesh*) does not mean what it means in Genesis 2:7, where God formed man of the *dust* of the ground, breathed into him the *breath* or spirit of life, and man became a living *soul.* In Genesis and generally in the Old Testament *soul* is a composite or compound of clay and spirit, incarnate man. This is not true in I Samuel 2:35, for God is not a compound of earth and spirit. "What is in my heart and in my soul" refers to God's plans for the future. They cannot be emotions because the immutable God is *impassible* and no more has emotional ups and downs than he has arms and eyes.

II Samuel 7:3 Go, do all that is in your mind [King James: thine heart], for the Lord is with thee.

The King James is the accurate translation; the NAS is the correct interpretation. David had plans for building a temple. God, as we know, cancelled these plans, but nonetheless the contents of David's *heart* were architectural propositions.

Psalm 4:4 Meditate in your heart upon your bed and be still.

Here intellection is commanded and emotions are explicitly forbidden. Meditation is a strictly intellectual activity. It requires quiet and stillness. Emotion hinders, distorts, or almost eradicates thinking. Acting under the stress of emotion we usually act blindly. An emotionally overwrought student, having had a spat with his sweetheart, can't memorize the Greek irregular verbs or solve a problem in physics. Nor can he do theology. We must meditate and be still. This command displeases pragmatic Americans.

Psalm 7:10 Who saves the upright in heart.

The context rather clearly specifies righteous conduct; that is, the heart here chiefly refers to volition. Unhypocritical assent to God's commands is presupposed as a background.

Psalm 12:2 They speak falsehoods to one another; with flattering lips and with a double heart they speak.

Obviously this is an intellectual activity. The *heart*, that is, the intellect, has devised false statements for the purpose of flattering. To utilize deceit requires at least a modicum of intelligence. Also note the contrast between the *lips* and at least one *heart*, the heart that knows its purpose and recognizes the falsehoods.

Psalm 14:1 The fool hath said in his heart, There is no God.

The man may be a fool for thinking so, but nonetheless he *thinks* in his heart—it is the *heart* that thinks. The context which follows speaks of corrupt and abominable deeds, but these have their origin in the heart that thinks.

Psalm 15:2 He who . . . speaks truth in his heart.

Unlike the fool of Psalm 14, the man here thinks and speaks the truth. The remainder of the Psalm describes some of his actions, none of which is emotional. He speaks to himself in his heart and what he says is the truth. The term *heart* obviously means the mind or intellect.

Isaiah 6:10 Make the heart of this people dull . . . and their eyes dim . . . lest they see with their eyes . . . understand with their heart, and repent and be healed.

Explicitly the heart is here described as the organ of understanding. Repentance, mentioned in the final phrase, is a change of mind. How can so many preachers who claim to be Biblical have missed so much in the Old Testament? They speak with devout fervor, but their message owes more to Freud than to the Scriptures. Also note parenthetically that the *eyes* mentioned here are not the two orbs in the front of the face. It is not sensation that is alluded to; the seeing is also an intellectual seeing, as when one "sees" the solution of a problem.

Isaiah 10:7 [God uses Assyria for his own purpose] Yet it does not so intend, nor does it plan so in its heart.

The General Staff of the Assyrian Army works out military plans in its heart. It is unaware that God is using them for his purpose. Nevertheless they do the planning and thinking in their hearts. This takes intelligence. The heart therefore is the mind or intellect.

Isaiah 33:18 Your heart will meditate on terror.

Not only is meditation referred to the heart, but the context specifies counting and weighing. This heart will no longer be baffled by "unintelligible speech which no one comprehends or a stammering tongue which no one understands." Presumably the converse, comprehension and understanding, will be the case. This is what the heart does.

> Isaiah 44:18, 19 They do not know nor do they understand, for he has smeared over their eyes so that they cannot see and their hearts so that they cannot comprehend. . . . Nor is there knowledge or understanding.

Note again that the *eyes* and the *seeing* have nothing to do with literal sensation, but with comprehension. The Scriptural evidence that the term *heart* means the mind, the intellect, the understanding, is becoming tedious in length. But the emotional error is so widespread that it ought to be buried under a thousand verses. We shall, however, add only another half dozen to the Old Testament list.

> Jeremiah 3:17 Nor shall they walk any more after the stubbornness of their evil heart. 5:23, 24 A stubborn and rebellious heart . . . they do not say in their heart, Let us now fear the Lord our God. 9:26 Uncircumcised of heart. 23:16 They speak a vision [revelation] of their own heart.

The last of these references envisages the mind or understanding. The others seem to refer more directly to the will or volition. Yet there can be no volition without a prior intellection.

> Zechiariah 7:10 Do not devise evil in your hearts.

Jeremiah 3:17 More directly indicated the volition, with the understanding presupposed. This verse indicates the intellect, with later volition implied.

Now, just in case some enthusiastic evangelist should say that the emotional New Testament contradicts and supersedes the intellectual Old Testament, we shall supply another tedious list.

Matthew 5:8 Blessed are the pure in heart. 5:28 . . . has committed adultery with her already in his heart.

If these two verses do not clearly refer to intellection or comprehension, they at least and clearly enough refer to volition. Even if adultery includes emotions, as it does, the emphasis here is on the decision or volition.

Matthew 6:21 Where your treasure is, there will your heart be also.

Depositing one's treasure in a safe place requires first a judgment of evaluation and then a volition that places the treasure there. Depositing one's pay check in a bank is not usually an emotional affair.

Matthew 9:4 Wherefore think ye evil in your hearts?

The men whom Jesus here castigates had been guilty of drawing some invalid inferences. Their inferences were indeed fallacious, or at least based on a false premise; but their activity was nonetheless ratiocination.

Matthew 11:29 I am meek and lowly of heart.

In this situation emotion is completely ruled out. Meekness and lowliness do not comport with emotional outbreaks. The mind must be calm.

Matthew 12:34, 40 Out of the abundance of the heart the mouth speaks . . . for as Jonah was three days and three nights . . . so shall the Son of Man be in the heart of the earth.

Verse 40 is quoted here to show how the term *heart* can be used metaphorically, and also because the list is to contain every instance of Matthew's use of the word. This assumes that the term is missing from verse 35. It is verse 34 that advances the argument. When a man thinks, meditates, ponders, and arrives at well-thought-out ideas, he speaks them. He speaks with his mouth, but the organ of thinking is the heart.

> Matthew 13:15, 19 This people's heart is waxed gross [NAS: has become dull] . . . lest they should understand with their heart. . . . When anyone hears the word of the kingdom and does not understand it, the evil one comes and snatches away what has been sown in his heart.

Could it be any more clearly expressed that understanding is the function of the heart? Someone hears the gospel for the first time and does not understand it. The words remain in the mind for a time; but since he does not understand, the evil one easily erases even the words.

> Matthew 15:8, 18, 19 This people . . . honoreth me with their lips, but their heart is far from me. . . . Those things which proceed out of the mouth come forth from the heart . . . for out of the heart come evil thoughts, murders . . . .

The contrast of verse 18 is that between the heart and the lips. It is not the now popular contrast between the head and the heart. The people in question are hypocrites. After a short conversation with his disciples Jesus, speaking more generally, teaches that what a man says originates in his heart. This is true even of the hypocrite, for he has already thought in his heart that it would be best to say what he does not believe. Thus, though he speaks well, he plans murder in his heart. Emotions do not plan murder.

> Matthew 18:35 If ye from your hearts forgive not . . .

Jesus here contrasts, at least by implication, an insincere forgiveness with a sincere forgiveness. One might speak words of forgiveness, yet harbor deep resentment. To forgive from the heart indicates a forgiveness that is one's basic intent and thought: the words correctly represent the mind. The heart is the mind.

Matthew 22:37 Thou shalt love the Lord thy God with all thy heart, and with all thy soul, and with all thy mind.

This is not a metaphysical trichotomous theory of human personality. The three terms are synonymous, joined together for emphasis. They do not separate the heart and the mind: They identify them.

Matthew 24:48 If that evil slave says in his heart . . .

Here the slave, having concluded that his master will not return for a long time, hatches a plan to defraud the inferior slaves. He hatches this plan in his heart. He has thought out all or most of the details. The function of the heart is to think and plan. The heart is the intellect.

This has been, I believe, a complete list of every instance of the term *heart* in Matthew's Gospel. Confused Calvinists should now adjust the thoughts of their hearts to conform with Scripture, even if Arminians find it impossible to do so.

But wait. It may resemble continuing blows on one who is already knocked out on the canvas, but some later books of the New Testament must be mentioned.

The Book of Acts contains about twenty instances of the word *heart*. The first occurrence is in 2:26 and can very plausibly refer to the emotions. It is quite true that the term *heart* in a few instances refers to the emotions. In the same chapter, verse 37, "pierced to the heart," or "smitten in conscience," may include a tinge of emotion, and verse 46, "gladness and sincerity of heart" may have an emotional overtone.

Acts 4:32 concerns a judgment on economic policy that

eventually became a disappointment; while Acts 5:3, 4 refer to the heart of Ananias as having planned to lie to the Holy Ghost. It was a deliberate economic planning, an activity of the mind, without a trace of emotion. In Acts 7:23 Moses, when forty years of age, decided—"it entered his heart"—to inspect the condition of the Jews in Egyptian slavery. This was a considered political step that turned out otherwise than Moses had planned. Verses 39 and 51 also refer to political planning, with a religious decision involved in the latter verse. Acts 8:21, 22 as well refer to personal gain or prestige; no emotional element is obvious. Acts 8:37, even if spurious, is still Greek, and it identifies the function of the heart as believing that Jesus Christ is the Son of God. This is a theological judgment. There are eight additional instances of the term *heart* in Acts, and the reader is encourged to look them up.

Romans seems to have fifteen instances of the term. In Romans 1:21 the heart is connected with a false theology, and three verses later this results in immorality. The immorality included sexual emotions, but it also included idolatry and the worship of animals. This is theology too. Romans 2:5 refers to an unrepentant heart, more theological than emotional; Romans 2:15, as I see it, asserts certain apriori principles derived from the creation of Adam. This is the structure of the human mind. The last verse of the chapter contrasts purely external conformity with religious tradition versus the sincere theology of a regenerate Israelite. There is an intellectual difference.

Some people may want to see emotions in Romans 5:5. It would be hard to prove. Romans 6:17, speaking of obedience, uses the term *heart* for volition. Romans 8:27 is another instance. If "unceasing grief" is indeed an emotion, then 9:2 uses the word in this sense. But I cannot see that "my heart's desire and prayer" in 10:1 is an emotion. It is rather a fixed determination. The instances in 10:6, 8, 9, 10 are indisputably intellectual, or volitional in the assent of verses 9 and 10. The final reference in Romans is 16:18 in which the subject is intellectual deception.

First Corinthians has five references: 2:9; 4:5; 7:37 twice; and 14:25. The first of these refers to theological doctrines underivable in empirical philosophy, but received, understood, and believed through revelation. Note the emphasis on mind (Greek *nous*) at the end of the chapter. I Corinthians 4:5 has nothing to do with emotion. Chapter 7:37 refers to a principle of parental control; and 14:25 concerns a knowledge of one's previous conduct, now recognized as sinful.

If any reader finds this list tedious, let him consider how tedious it is for the present author to check it out and write it down. The term *heart* occurs about 160 times in the New Testament. The instances now given, both from Old and New, conclusively show that the basic meaning of the word is mind or intellect. Volition, usually the assent to intellectually understood propositions, is also a meaning, and emotion is rarely the point of the passage. Suppose we agree not to complete the enumeration, but just stop right here.

Before the intrusion of this material on the head and the heart, the argument had begun with "two or three difficulties in this section from Calvin:" first, the unfortunate behavioristic overtones of some of Calvin's language; second, the defective grasp of Biblical psychology in many writers; and now we proceed to the third point. The context in Calvin from which the unfortunate language was quoted insists that "it is an absurdity to say that faith is formed by the addition of a pious affection to an assent of the mind; whereas even this assent is a pious affection." Calvin uses the term *affection* to denote a voluntary intellectual assent. Not all assents are pious. Not only may one assent, unknowingly, to a falsehood; but also an assent to a proposition of geometry is not a "pious" assent. Here Hodge with many others confuses the nature of the assent with the propositions assented to.

The effect, indeed the unwitting acknowledgment, of this type of confusion comes on the next page. "That saving faith is not a mere speculative assent of the understanding, is the uniform doctrine of the Protestant symbols. On this point, however, it may be remarked, in the first place, that . . . the Scriptures do not make the sharp distinction between the understanding, the feelings, and the will, which is common today" (p. 91). Is this not an acknowledgment that Hodge and others have imposed a foreign psychology on the Scripture? Hodge continues, "A large class of our inward acts and states are so complex as to be acts of the whole soul, and not exclusively of any one of its faculties." Here again the distinctions are assigned in the wrong direction. Faculty psychology, largely abandoned now, invented parts or faculties of the soul for various acts, while the Scripture, as I understand it, has the unitary soul or mind acting on various objects. For example, conscience is not a faculty of the soul for morality and intellect a separate faculty for geometry. Rather the distinction is that in the first case the mind studies matters of morality, while in the second the same unitary mind studies geometry. This view is consonant with the idea that faith in pickles and faith in God are psychologically identical; the difference lies in the object. If, further, the older term *affection* (which in Greek used to mean something like being hit with a hammer) means what we today call *emotion*, it must be described as a sudden disturbance in the mind's normal intelligence. Most sins, perhaps not all, occur because an emotion has disturbed the mind's rationality. That is why the New Testament so often condemns desire or lust.

Hodge's account of faith, though deformed by his empiri-

cal philosopy, is nonetheless correct in the main. The same
page continues, "If we take that element of faith, which is
common to every act of believing, if we understand by it the
apprehension of a thing as true and worthy of confidence . . .
then it may be said that faith in its essential nature is intellectual or intelligent assent." Granted, Hodge does not finish his
paragraph consistently, but his final words, if we take the term
*heart* in its scriptural sense, are good: "the faith that is required
for salvation is an act of the whole soul, of the understanding,
of the heart, and of the will" (p. 91). All that remains to be done
is to clarify the relation between the understanding and the
will, which together are actions of the heart or mind.

# 10. B.B. Warfield

The great Princeton Warfield[18] begins his chapter on faith
with a study of the Hebrew word we may transliterate into the
English *Amen*, which the verb *believe* in the King James uniformly represents. Yet he says that *believe* is a weaker and
dilute meaning of the Hebrew verb. The stronger meanings
denote fixedness, steadfastness, and reliability. Just why
*fixedness* is *strong* and *believe* is *weak*, Warfield does not
explain. The Hiphil form of the verb, with one exception,
means " 'to trust,' weakening down to the simple 'to believe.' "
With the prefix *beth*, "It is probably never safe to represent the
phrase by the simple 'believe' " (p. 468). Warfield, without
denying that the object of this verb can be a theological proposition, stresses a personal object more than Hodge did. He
repeats the unfortunate pejorative claim that "This faith . . . is

18. "The Biblical Doctrine of Faith." in *Biblical Doctrine* (Oxford University Press,
1929), pp. 467-508.

obviously no mere assent" (p. 470). Yet to do him justice one must note also that "The thing believed is sometimes a specific word or work of God . . . the fact of a divine revelation . . . or the words or commandments of God in general," as well as "God's prophets" and "God himself." He rather stresses the latter, for he continues: "The object of Abram's faith . . . was not the promise . . . what it [Abram's faith] rested on was God himself. . . . To believe in God, in the Old Testament sense, is thus not merely [pejorative] to assent to His word, but . . . to rest . . . upon Him" (p. 471).

Warfield then tries to preserve this alleged Hebrew meaning for the Greek *pisteuo* (believe) by connecting the latter to the former through the usage of the Septuagint. This background in the Septuagint was necessary because "it [*pisteuo*] had the slightest possible connection with religious faith in classical speech" (p. 472). Here again is the confusion of meaning with the object. Had *pisteuo* in classical Greek a strong religious connotation, its meaning might have been too much colored by pagan superstitions. But without such pagan connotations its common usage can be taken over in the New Testament. Indeed, Warfield's attempt to justify his view by an appeal to Xenophon's *Memorabilia* undermines rather than establishes his position. If the Greek *pisteuein* was so far removed from the Old Testament *Amen,* how was it that the Seventy chose it as the best translation?

Similarly his argument based on Philo's use of *pistis* (faith) is vitiated by the same confusion. Philo's *faith* may have been naturalistic, not even synergistic, while New Testament faith is a gift of God's grace; but these differences are irrelevant. We are not here concerned with the cause of faith, nor with the different objects of faith, but with the nature of faith. Whether Zeus or Jehovah, whether botany or astronomy or mathematics be the object, the question is, Is faith an *assent*? Note too that any pagan influence that Philo might have absorbed—less than many people think—could not have affected the Seventy, who came about two hundred years earlier.

But for all Warfield's aversion from assent, he clearly admits that "When construed with the dative, *pisteuein* in the New Testament prevailingly expresses believing assent, though ordinarily in a somewhat pregnant sense," whatever this last phrase may mean. "When its object is a thing, it is usually the spoken . . . or written . . . word of God" (p. 475). With respect to *pisteuein* and the accusative he says, "With these weaker [why weaker?] constructions must be ranged also the passages, twenty in all . . . in which what is believed is joined to the verb by the conjunction *oti.*"

A "deeper sense of the word" is indicated when the verb is followed by prepositions, even though the preposition in Mark 1:15 governs the "gospel" (p. 476). There are of course many instances when the grammatical object is a person. The exegesis of these passages has already been hinted at and will be further discussed later.

When Warfield takes up "The Historical Presentation of Faith," he acknowledges that "the first recorded acts after the Fall—the naming of Eve, and the birth and naming of Cain—are expressive of trust in God's promise" (p. 485). In the following sentence he speaks of Noah's "trust in God and His promises." At least twice on page 486 he describes the patriarchal religion as a "religion of promise." It is impossible for any honest student of the Old Testament to avoid the idea of promise, and this requires the object of faith to be a proposition. Continuing his historical survey Warfield writes, "The law-giving was not a setting aside of the religion of promise" (p. 486).

It is necessary to remind the reader that these criticisms of Warfield and other Calvinistic theologians with reference to

the nature of faith as assent do not derogate from the excel-
lence of their exposition of Biblical faith as soteric, as an
endowment from God, and whatever force and value the Scriptures assign to it. The point of the criticism is that these
spiritual qualities belong to an act of assent, rather than to a
very vague something else. This confusion mars Warfield's
otherwise fine discussion of faith in James (p. 495). Contrary to
what he says, James did not "rebuke the Jewish tendency to
conceive faith . . . as a mere [the pejorative word again] intellectual acquiescence." In addition to Warfield's pointing out
that James wrote, "If a man *say* he have faith, can the [that sort
of] faith save him?" one must note that their "intellectual
acquiescence" had a different object; and it was the difference
in object, not the similarity in intellectual assent, that deprived
their faith of soteric efficacy. Warfield also falls into the error
of supposing that Hebrews 11:1 is the *definition* of faith (p.
498), while the remainder of the chapter is a *description*. It is all
a description. And it is incredible that he says, "Least of all the
New Testament writers could John confine faith to a merely [!]
intellectual act: his whole doctrine is rather a protest against
the intellectualism of Gnosticism" (p. 500). Warfield seems to
suppose that if John combatted the intellectualism of the
Gnostics, he had to oppose all intellectualism.[19]

In his final section on "The Biblical Conception of Faith"
Warfield again takes Hebrews 11:1 as "almost [!] a formal
definition . . . it consists neither in assent nor in obedience" (p.
501). But try as he may to make God rather than a proposition
the object of faith, he must include a belief in "the forgiveness

---

19. As for John's intellectualism, see *The Johannine Logos*, and my commentary on
*First John*, Jefferson, Maryland: The Trinity Foundation. These two and the one on
*Colossians* also present a view of the relationship between Christianity and Gnosticism
rather different from the view popular in Warfield's day.

of sins . . . the revelations of this grace, and the provisions of
this mercy" (p. 502). These terms indicate certain propositions
to be believed, accepted as true, given our assent. "Such a faith,
again, could not fail to embrace with humble confidence all the
gracious promises [!] of the God of salvation . . . nor could it
fail to lay hold with strong conviction [though one man said,
Lord, I believe, help thou my unbelief] on all [does anyone
know them all?] those revealed truths . . ." (p. 503). Nonetheless a few lines farther down the page he denies that faith
terminates on the promise, namely, those "propositions which
declare God's grace and willingness to save."

## 11. Minor Men

During the life time of Charles Hodge, John Anderson
wrote a good book on *Saving Faith*.[20] A short summary will be
sufficient to outline his views. "He who is the object of our faith
is called Christ" (p. 18). There follow several pages on the
offices of Christ. Coming to the object of faith he asks,
"Whether such principles as the being of God, the immortality
of the soul, a future state of rewards and punishments, as they
are known by human reason in its present corrupt state, are to
be considered as objects of faith?" And he answers, "It is
absurd to call such truths . . . objects or matters of faith, while
they are known and considered no otherwise than as matters of
reason" (p. 31). Note the phrase, "as they are known by human
reason in its present corrupt state." This phrase prevents the
passage from being pertinent to the question of this study. It
even seems as if Dr. Anderson thinks it possible to prove the

---

20. Pittsburgh, Pennsylvania: United Presbyterian Board of Publication, Fifth ed.
1875.

truth of these propositions by "human reason" (never defined) apart from revelation. For example, he speaks of "These truths, not as matters of faith, but as dictates of reason . . . and whoever is an enemy [of these "rational" truths] must be much more an enemy of the latter [truths of revelation]" (pp. 22, 23). Of course this is false, as anyone with a knowledge of Aquinas, or of non-thomistic presuppositionalists, recognizes.

More to the point for the present study, Anderson acknowledges that "The whole word of God is indeed the object of faith . . . [though] in the word, which is its general object, it seeks a special object" (p. 38).

In Discourse II Anderson examines "the ACT of believing in the name of Jesus Christ, abstracted from such things as accompany or follow it" (p. 46). This faith is not "a resolved subjection to, or compliance with, what they call the precepts of the gospel" (p. 50). "The following [is the] definition of saving faith: 'that it is a real or unfeigned persuasion, wrought in my heart by the Holy Ghost, that, in the gospel record, . . . God gives his Son Jesus Christ, with his whole salvation, to sinners of mankind indefinitely, and to me a sinner in particular' " (p. 54).

How much of the record one must believe, he does not say; and unless *I* know what to believe, how can I know that anything applies to *me*? On the following page he seems to include the knowledge of "the all-sufficiency of his Son Jesus to accomplish our salvation." Since this requires several pages to explain, including 20-25 Scripture verses, from the Old Testament as well as from the New, the object to be believed seems to be a somewhat extensive theology. Indeed, Scriptural exposition continues for pages, and there is no clear indication of how much is essential to saving faith. In this exposition, too, the *act* of faith, though it was the chapter heading, seems to have been forgotten. But he returns to it on page 82.

He states, "To consider the ACT of saving faith . . . we must observe that it is a persuasion wrought in our hearts by the supernatural operation of the Holy Spirit. . . . Secondly, we observe that it is a SURE persuasion . . . it must carry in it real assurance" (p. 83). Though this contradicts the Westminster Confession, he continues saying that "true and saving faith evidences assurance to be its nature" (p. 84). It is "a belief of the gospel record" (p. 86). It includes "all the purposes of Justification and salvation." Then later he adds, "There is an appropriation in nature of saving faith, from its correspondence with the record of God concerning his Son Jesus Christ" (p. 121). "Faith is further distinguished . . . by its hearty approbation of . . . the whole device of salvation through Christ crucified, as well ordered in all things and sure" (p. 129). This surely takes in a great amount of theology.

Anderson frequently mentions belief in the promise. A promise, and the particular promise he mentions of a son to Abram, is a proposition; but he does not specify any particular promise to us, speaking only generally of "the word of the gospel" (p. 137). "The appropriation . . . arises from the matter believed, or from the records that God hath given us . . ." (p. 146). "Strong faith . . . is that which proceeds most singly upon the ground of God's word of promise" (p. 146). This is in general true, and in the main Anderson seems to hold that the object of faith is propositional.

Johan H. Bavinck, another minor writer, is the author of a book whose title is *Faith and Its Difficulties.*[21] It may not be his best work, but its title brings it within the scope of this investigation.

A man's publications must in some way reveal what we may call his psychological constitution. Bavinck's is evident on

21. Grand Rapids, Michigan: Wm. B. Eerdmans, Company, 1959.

his first page: "One is possessed with a feeling of awe when one begins to talk about God." Perhaps this ought to be so. Trying to imagine what that omnipotence is which could create ex nihilo the galaxies astronomy talks about, should discourage us from trying to imagine. But Bavinck's anxiety before God seems to stem from a less justifiable anxiety before his human friends: "Even when I talk with a friend about my fellow man, who has the same peculiarities and weaknesses that I have, I realize that at any moment I run the danger of doing him an injustice . . . that I will attribute ulterior motives, while in reality there are none." Though this is a danger in published works—I have misrepresented D'Arcy by summarizing only a part of his book—and while the attribution of ulterior motives of others than authors is possible, it occurs in only a small, a very small proportion of conversations, and is certainly not an important factor to govern a study of faith. But Bavinck is so gripped by anxiety he denies what many Reformed theologians assert, namely, that we can think God's thoughts after him. After denying this he adds, "I am convinced that no language has the word power adequately to express the ineffable majesty of His Being. We wish to speak about the unknown God" (p. 9).

Since language is a gift from God with the purpose of enabling us to speak about him and to him, and since the Bible contradicts the idea of God's being unknown or "totally other," Bavinck's theory of language should be viewed with suspicion. Of course no one denies that we are ignorant of what God has not chosen to reveal. The well-known verse in Deuteronomy (29:29) is explicit and in thinking it we think that thought of God after him. Further, if God is unknown, there is no good reason for writing a book on faith. Even if we often misunderstand, yet we must sometimes get the truth, for that is why God gave us a book that is profitable for (true) doctrine, for reproof, and instruction in righteousness. Even when Bavinck acknowledges that "This does not mean that there is no way by which we may learn to know him," he adds that for many people of our generation "He is nothing else but the UNKNOWN." Granted, he does not use the term *unknowable* in this sentence; but he has capitalized UNKNOWN, and this after saying that language is (inherently) inadequate.

Bavinck of course wants to make this unknown God somewhat knowable. "Nature's overwhelming greatness" leads man "irresistibly . . . forced to confess that there must be SOMETHING," though "Nature in itself is an unfathomable riddle. . . . That God of nature is for us the Unknown God." Then "guidance and direction" occurs to us on our "good days and bad days . . . and in all these things the great Ruler of our lives speaks to us." He is now seen as "the Regent of our life." Finally "we meet God . . . in Jesus Christ." Then apparently by faith we merge the SOMETHING, the Regent, and Christ into one. But still "we shudder at the appalling unknowness of God." Bavinck speaks of being "Oppressed with fear and anguish," and he "shudders." Several times he uses the phrase "the mysterious Other."

Can such a disturbed mentality give us a clear concept of faith?

Of course Bavinck believes that this Unknown Something has spoken in Jesus Christ. But if language is inadequate, do Christ's words give us any knowledge? Are Christ's words only unintelligible pointers to Something that soothes our disturbing emotions? Bavinck indeed says that "God revealed his eternal and holy will of salvation through the Cross of Christ" (p. 27). But is the Cross a symbol, a myth, or inexplicable fact? Or did God through Matthew, Paul, and John give an intelligible explanation of the significance of Christ's death? And do we, when we read words, obtain knowledge thereby? Bavinck presumably believes that Christ's death was a vicarious and

propitiatory sacrifice, but these pages do not show how his
presuppositions justify the possibility of such information.

A few pages later he gives other criteria of faith: "If the
palace of Caiaphas would have collapsed in the night of Jesus'
condemnation, or if Pilate had been struck dead in the midst of
the hearing—faith would not be faith anymore. . . . Everyone
would be forced to bend and give in. The facts would force us,
against our wills, to agree with God" (p. 28). This is unsatisfac-
tory for several reasons. First, there is still no definition of
faith. Second, in Old Testament times there were events as
spectacular as the collapse of Caiaphas' palace would have
been, and it was not true that "faith would not be faith any
more." Third, Jesus said that even if some people would return
from hell and tell their brothers of the penalties beyond the
grave, they would not "be forced against (their) wills to agree
with God." An author should not allow fervent devotion or
literary charm to hide the truth. On the next page (p. 29),
Bavinck describes a mustard seed as something "infinitesimally
small," which visibly it isn't. Now, no doubt some readers will
consider such objections as nit-picking. Yet it is not an infinitesimally small point: It is symptomatic of carelessness. If, however, I seem severe, let me say that pages 33-36, though too
rhetorical to suit my taste, are nonetheless very true.

Eventually Bavinck gives what seems to be intended as a
definition of faith: "Faith really is nothing else but the courageous decision that I will no more indulge in self-contemplation and speculation" (p. 45). Obviously this statement is
unacceptable. First, it does not apply to many of the beliefs
which the secular writers enumerate. Nor is it biblical. Surely
to confess that Jesus is the Messiah and that God raised him
from the dead is more than "nothing else but a courageous
decision . . . no more [to] indulge in self-contemplation." Not
only is there something else, but what Bavinck says is excluded

is actually included, unless self-examination, which Scripture commands, is not self-contemplation.

The remainder of the book leads to our conclusion that its title is a misnomer. It deals with cares of temptation and spiritual struggle, but has little to do with faith. As such it probes the sinful tendencies of even the best Christians and may prove of great help to many people. But it will impede rather than enlarge one's understanding of the gospel message.

## 12. John Theodore Mueller

After the earlier sections of this study, sections on secular views of belief, and after the Roman Catholic views, the material has been limited to the Calvinistic tradition. Obviously the present writer is a Calvinist, writing chiefly for Calvinists, with some pious hopes that others also may be influenced. Now, there is nothing wrong in confining one's attention to Calvinism. But since it was Luther, and not Calvin, who first brought the doctrine of justification by faith to the attention of Europe, and since Lutheranism is the numerically largest division of evangelicalism, we ought gratefully to acknowledge the fact, even though the reference be inadequate. John Theodore Mueller is a recent and excellent Lutheran theologian. In his *Systematic Theology* (p. 325) he uses the common three-fold division of knowledge, assent, and confidence. But he seems—and this puzzles a reader—to restrict knowledge and assent to uninterpreted historical events. Surely he cannot have meant this, for obviously a person can believe a doctrine as well as an historical event. Some modification, fortunately, occurs on the next page, where he says, "However, if the term *notitia* is understood in the sense of true spiritual knowledge of Christ . . . and the term *assensus* is conceived as spiritual assent to the promises of the Gospel . . . then both of these terms include the *fiducia cordis.*"

This, of course, makes *fiducia* redundant.

Even on the puzzling page he said, "Faith which justifies is not merely a knowledge of history . . . but it is assent to the promise of God. . . ." And two pages earlier (p. 323) he had asserted, "Saving faith is always *fides actualis* [not the Romish implicit faith], or the apprehension of the divine promise by an act of the intellect and will."

Though we hold Martin Luther in highest honor, later Lutheranism has been more Melanchthonian than Lutheran. Even so, the Missouri Synod and Concordia Seminary are to be admired for turning back the assaults of liberalism in the past decade. Yet, if the present study has taken some Calvinists to task on this or that point, it is permissible to state some difficulties found in Professor Mueller's learned tome. These difficulties are not so much located in the psychology of believing, for Mueller is very clear on the basic evangelical doctrine of assent, widely forgotten by non-lutherans who still call themselves evangelicals. The difference to be noted in the interest of a more balanced though still inadequate presentation has to do with the permanence of belief.

At first sight Mueller seems to be very Calvinistic. He writes, "It is clear that a believer is in full possession of divine pardon, life, and salvation from the very moment in which he puts his trust in Christ. . . . For this reason the believer is also certain of his salvation, for saving faith is in its very nature the truest and greatest certainty. If [any groups] deny that the believer may be sure of his salvation, it is because they teach that salvation in part at least depends upon the believer's good works . . ." (p. 329).

These words could easily be taken to imply the Calvinistic doctrine of the perseverance of the saints, if not that of irresistible grace. But later, on page 436, Mueller denies that all persevere and rejects Calvin's teaching that faith cannot be lost. "The Calvinistic doctrine of final perseverance is unscriptural" (p. 437). "Calvinism cannot comfort a believer with real assurance of salvation" (p.

438). Yet, strange to say, on the next page (p. 439) he states that "As God did not omit anything to prepare salvation for [the believer], so also he omits nothing by which this salvation is *finaliter* attained."

Now, an astute theologian may see more clearly than a layman who would be deceived how this wording can escape Calvinism. Even some Arminians assert assurance—in the sense that they are sure they would be taken to heaven if they should die right now, though if they live longer they may lose their faith and be lost. Similarly Mueller said, "Every true believer in Christ therefore is sure of his [present!] state of grace and salvation" (p. 332). But many of us will indeed live until tomorrow. Therefore Mueller's rejection of Calvinistic comfort cannot be of much comfort to Lutherans.


# 13. The End of History

Some of the more professorial readers of this book may be disappointed that so little attention is paid to current authors and so much to earlier theologians. There is a simple explanation. The earlier theologians, as the quotations indicate, wrote rather extensively on the subject, whereas during the second and third quarters of this century the material has been shorter in length and poorer in quality. One example illustrates both deficiencies. In *The Presbyterian Journal* (November 26, 1980) a contributor had an article entitled "Justification—Faith and Works." Particularly noticeable is the writer's failure to define his terms. To quote:

"The message of James becomes especially important when the teaching of bare faith-justification, or even assent-justification, arises to trouble the church, as it evidently was doing in his day, and as it is certainly doing in ours. This is the view that justifying faith does not necessarily include obedience or good works.

"The man who relies on assent-justification claims he has justifying faith when what he has is no more than intellectual assent to the Gospel and a desire to escape eternal damnation. The one who relies on assent-justification says, 'I accept Christ as Savior, but not yet as Lord.' He thinks he is assured of salvation because he has faith, but he does not understand what faith truly is.

"To understand the words of James, 'a man is justified by works,' to mean no more than that he demonstates his justification by his works, leaves the one who relies on assent-justification a false way of feeling that all is well with his soul."

In addition to his loose terminology the writer depends on false assertions. The end of the first quoted paragraph insists that 'assent-justification' "does not necessarily include obedience or good works." The word *necessarily* perhaps saves the paragraph from being outright false, provided the writer can quote an exponent of assent who explicitly says that good works are not included. Or, perhaps the truth of the statement can be defended by insisting that those who defend assent do not *include* good works in assent—they only say that good works follow. But without even this excuse the next to last sentence in paragraph two, namely, "The one who relies on assent-justification says, 'I accept Christ as Savior, but not yet as Lord,' " cannot escape the charge of outright falsehood. None of the Calvinistic theologians quoted above ever said any such thing. It is regrettable that a periodical, supposedly Calvinistic, should print such incompetent drivel. The Apostle Paul in his day met the essentially similar objection that justification by faith alone encouraged immorality. He defended his position in Romans VI, VII, and VIII.


## 14. The Necessity of Faith

To this point the discussion has been centered on the history of the doctrine. The objections to some parts of the various views, though in appearance negative, were, as earlier indicated, actually positive and constructive. Turning now from the historical matrix, the study will try to collect and somewhat organize these previous conclusions. Then, too, although there was a section on Biblical Data, more Biblical data are to be added. To begin with, a relatively non-controversial point will be made, not only to round out the exposition, but also because it leads into a most embarrassing puzzle. The thesis is that faith is necessary to salvation.

One difficulty in the doctrine of justification by faith alone has to do with infants and imbeciles. Most Christians believe that some who die in infancy are saved, and many believe that all who die in infancy are saved. But if faith is necessary, and if infants are incapable of believing anything, what happens to Calvinistic theology? The usual answer is to deny that faith is universally necessary and that infants and some others are justified without faith. The Lutherans, however, are more consistent. They hold that infants can exercise faith even before birth. Of course, how they can believe the gospel which they cannot possibly have heard remains a mystery, for the Scripture says, Faith cometh by hearing. On the other hand, Lutherans have a powerful point in their favor as they cite the case of John the Baptist, who was filled with the Holy Ghost while yet in his mother's womb.

The anti-christian Supreme Court should consider this when they legalize the murder of babies on the ground that they are not yet human beings.

Be this all as it may, Supreme Court, Calvinism, and Lutheranism, each reader must decide for himself whether the following Biblical passages require the conclusion that faith is a necessity for salvation. And if faith is necessary to salvation, it is necessary for theology also. We must understand what the Scriptures say. The following verses, or at least some of them, seem to teach that faith is necessary. Assuredly they teach more than this, and references to them must later be made in explanation of other phases of the doctrine. But they are given here for the sole purpose of pointing out the necessity of faith.

John 3:15, 16 Everyone who believes in him has everlasting life . . . He who believes in him shall not perish.

Acts 16:31 Believe on the Lord Jesus, and thou shalt be saved.

Strictly speaking these two verses do not show that faith is necessary to salvation. They show that faith is sufficient. If someone believes, he has eternal life. No one is lost who believes. But these two verses, if taken alone, allow for the possibility that something else could be substituted for faith. Suppose I am driving south on Interstate 65, and in Kentucky I come to Cave City. The attendant at the gas station says, "If you take routes 9 and 231 you will surely get to Murphreesboro." True enough. But it is also true that if I continue on I-65 and 24 I shall get to Murphreesboro just as well. Now . . .

Mark 16:16 He who believes and is baptized shall be saved, but he who does not believe shall be condemned.

teaches not only that faith is sufficient, but also that without faith salvation is impossible. However, since some scholars do not regard this as part of the canon, three other verses follow.

James 3:18 He who believes in him is not judged; he who does not believe is judged already.

James 3:36 He who believes in the Son has eternal life; but he who disobeys the Son shall not see life.

Hebrews 11:6 Without faith it is impossible to please [God]."

These verses are sufficiently explicit; but the general doctrine of justification by faith alone is a stronger proof than a few sample verses. The passages on justification may not singly be so explicit:

It is necessary to combine them and draw inferences. But in view of the last half of Romans 3, and for that matter of the last half of Romans 5, the conclusion is the more compelling because the base is broader.

## 15. The Language

Since faith is of such importance, and even if it were not of such importance, theology must determine its meaning. Those who wish to talk about it ought to know the nature of that particular kind of faith which is necessary for salvation. Herman Hoeksema (*Reformed Dogmatics*, Grand Rapids, 1966, p. 479) begins his chapter on Saving Faith with this paragraph: "Saving faith is that work of God in the elect, regenerated, and called sinner whereby the latter is ingrafted into Christ and embraces and appropriates Christ and all his benefits, relying upon him in time and eternity." Aside from the fact that some of the verbs in this sentence are too vague to be useful, one may admit that the sentence is true. But it is not a definition of faith. To say that faith ingrafts us into Christ says less than to say roast beef gives us nourishment. The latter does not tell us what beef is. Nor does the former tell us what faith is. Theological terms need to be defined; they need to be understood; or else we do not know what we are talking about. To make progress toward a definition, we begin with the usage of the language.

The Greek verb means *believe*. So it was translated in the previous verses quoted. Here will follow some instances of its ordinary use, both in pagan sources and in the Bible. The Biblical verses from the Septuagint are not chosen because they are Biblical, but, like the pagan sources, they show how the word was used in pre-christian times. When the New Testament authors began to write, they perforce used the common language.

Aristotle, *De Anima* 428 b 4: The sun is believed to be larger than the earth.

Aristotle, *Meteorologica* 343 b 10 [On a certain point] it is necessary to believe the Egyptians.

Thucydides I, 20, It is hard to believe every bit of evidence about them.

Psalm 78:22 in the Septuagint translation says that the Israelites "did not believe in God."

Isaiah 53:1 Who has believed our report?

Even though this is the common usage—and in a moment a large number of New Testament passages will show the same thing—a number of theologians give the impression that the translation *believe* is misleading. They want to make "faith" something other than "mere" belief. The following lengthy list has some bearing on this conviction.

John 2:22 They believed the Scripture.

John 3:12 If I told you about earthly matters and you do not believe, how shall you believe if I tell you about heavenly things?

John 4:50 The man believed the word that Jesus had spoken to him.

John 5:47 If ye believe not that man's writing, how shall ye believe my words?

John 6:69 We have believed and know that thou art the Holy One of God.

John 8:24 If ye believe not that I am (what I claim to be) ye shall die in your sins.

John 8:45 Because I tell you the truth, you do not believe me.

John 9:18 But the Jews did not believe . . . that he had

been blind.

John 11:26 Do you believe this?

27 Yes, Lord, I believe that thou art the Christ.

John 11:42 I said it that they may believe that thou hast sent me.

John 12:38 Who hath believed our report?

John 13:19 Ye may believe that I am he.

John 14:29 Now I have told you before it happens, so that when it happens you might believe.

John 16:27 And have believed that I came out from God.

John 16:30 We believe that thou camest forth from God.

John 17:8 have believed that thou didst send me.

John 17:21 that the world may believe that thou hast sent me.

John 20:31 These are written that you might believe that Jesus is the Christ, the Son of God.

I Corinthians 13:7 Love believes everything.


In reading over these verses carefully, the student should note that the object of the verb is sometimes a noun or pronoun denoting a statement (word, this, things, writings), and sometimes a person (in this list, *me*; in other verses *God*), and sometimes there is no explicit object at all. The significance of this will become apparent in a moment.

To be specific and to make the New Testament data clear, note that the object of belief in John 2:22 is the Scripture; in John 3:12, earthly and heavenly things, i.e., information concerning earthly and heavenly society; in John 4:50 the man believed the word, not a single word like *sun, rain,* or *Jerusalem,* but rather a sentence. The Greek word *logos* hardly ever means a single word, and the usual translation of John 1:1 is a mistake that has befuddled nearly everybody. In John 6:69 the object of the verb *believe* is the phrase "that thou art the Holy One of God." Other cases of *believe that* are John 8:24, 9:18, 11:27, and at least eight others in the list.

It is clear that the Greek verb *pisteuo* is properly translated *believe*; and it would have been much better if the noun *pistis* had been translated *belief.* An English novel, *The Way of All Flesh,* indicates that in the late eighteenth and early nineteenth centuries the evangelical Anglicans recited the *Belief,* rather than the *Creed.* The author seems to assume that the congregations did not know that *credo* means *I believe.* The partial examination of the verses just above shows what the object of belief is. Usually it is the truth. Even where the grammatical object is not a phrase, the sense requires it.

The Scriptures contain many instances of the verb with the noun *God* as their explicit object. Though none of the verses in the last group quoted has *God* as the explicit object, everyone remembers that "Abraham believed God." The verb here should not be taken to mean something different from its other instances. What Abraham believed was the promise of God. God said, "I am thy shield . . . This shall not be thine heir . . . So shall thy seed be. And he [Abraham] believed in the Lord"(Genesis 15:1-6); and "Abraham believed God"(Romans 4:3). In English too, when we say we believe a person, we mean we agree that his statement is true.

If this is now settled, still some people assert that there is a distinct and important difference between believing a statement or even believing a person and believing *in* a person.

Before the argument resumes, it is best to collect some more Scriptural data.

Matthew 18:6 and Mark 9:42 one of these little ones who believe in [*eis*] me.

John 1:12 He gave power to them who believe in [*eis*] his name.

John 2:11 His disciples believed in him.

John 2:23 Many believed on [*eis*] his name.

John 7:5 Neither did his brothers believe in him.

John 9:35-36 Do you believe on the Son of God . . . who is he, Lord, that I may believe on [*eis*] him.

John 12:36 Believe in [*eis*] the light.

John 14:1 Ye believe in [*eis*] God, believe also in me.

Acts 16:31 Believe on [*epi*] the Lord Jesus and thou shalt be saved and thy house.

Romans 4:18 Who against hope believed in [*epi*] hope.

I Timothy 1:16 Believe on [*epi*] him to life everlasting.

I Peter 1:21 Who are believers [noun] in God.

The first reference in this last list speaks of young children. They cannot have had much theological education. The passage of course does not mean that we should be like children in respect of their ignorance, nor, as is sometimes wrongly assumed, in respect of their innocence. But rather they believed that Jesus would somehow bless them. If anyone wish to say the children *trusted* in him, well and good; to trust is to believe *that* good will follow.

The contrast between John 2:11, 23 and John 7:5 is that some believed Jesus was the Messiah and some did not.

John 12:36 and its context speak of light. The light seems to be the Old Testament in verse 34. It may also be Christ's interpretation of the Old Testament prophecies. Later Christ would be taken away and the Old Testament would be darkness to them. Verses 35 and 36 need not be translated "*While* you have light," but equally good grammar allows "As you have light"; i.e., use whatever degree of light you now have.

Here, as often, the contrast between light and darkness is the
contrast between truth and falsehood.

The final verse in the list uses the noun *believers*, or a
substantive adjective if you wish. It does not mean trusting or
faithful; but believer. Acts 16:1 refers to Timothy's mother as a
believer (feminine form). Ephesians 1:1 is better translated "to
the believers in Christ Jesus," as also in Colossians 1:2 and a
dozen other places.

These references are cited because some people find a
great difference between believing a person and believing *in*
him. There is no doubt a difference, but it is quite different
from the difference these people think they have in mind.
Attentive readers who read their publications will conclude
that very likely they have nothing in mind, for they regularly
avoid stating what the difference is. Let us use a human example, for if we begin by talking about believing in God, our sense
of piety may deceive us. Any ordinary instance will do. I meet a
stranger on the plane and we begin to talk. His conversation
indicates that he is a chemical engineer. Somewhere along the
line he remarks that a certain chemical process does so and so. I
believe him; I accept his statement as true. But I do not for that
reason believe *in* him. He may be a scoundrel. Occasionally
engineers are. On the way home I sit next to a very good friend
of longstanding. He is a lawyer. He tells me about some legal
matter. But now I not only believe this one statement: I believe
*in* him because I believe that anything he will tell me in the
future, especially if it concerns law, will be true. I believe he
always tells the truth and always will. Of course, since he is a
human being, he may make a mistake. But when we believe *in*
God, we believe *that* he will never make a mistake. To believe *in*
is simply a reference to the future beyond the present single
statement.

Then too some preachers who have had a year or two of

Greek make allegedly scholarly remarks about a difference between a New Testament belief and a pagan Greek belief. A better scholar, Kittel (Vol. VI, pp. 203-208) has these things to say. "There is nothing distinctive in the NT usage . . . as compared with Greek usage. . . . *Pisteuein eis* is equivalent to *pisteuein oti*, to regard credible or true. *Pisteuein eis XJ* . . . simply means *pisteuein oti I. apethanen kai aneste*. . . . In John especially *pisteuein eis* and *pisteuein oti* are constantly used interchangeably. Compare also Acts 8:37 E[22]. . . . This is proved also by the passive expression *episteuthe* (cf. I Timothy 3:16) and the fact that *pistis eis* is equivalent, not to *pistis* c. dat. but to *pistis* c. gen obj. . . ."

Two pages later he says, "*Pisteuein* . . . often means to believe God's words. Belief is thus put in Scripture (James 2:22), in what is written in the Law, in what the prophets have said (Luke 24:25) . . . in Moses and his writings (James 5:46 ff.)." Compare also pp. 208, 222.

To translate or to summarize a little, Kittel said: To believe *in* is equivalent to believe *that*. To believe in Christ Jesus simply means to believe that Jesus died and rose again. In John especially *to believe in* and *to believe that* are constantly used interchangeably.

In opposition to Kittel's linguistic studies, some theologians and many ministers wish to minimize belief and detach faith from truth. Louis Berkhof strangely tends in this direction. Since at this time he commands widespread respect and since many schools use his book, it proves profitable to conclude this subsection with a few paragraphs concerning his views. The material comes from his *Systematic Theology*, fourth edition, 1969, Part IV, chapter 8, pp. 493 ff.

He admits that John 4:50 uses the verb *pisteuo* in the

---

22. Even if the verse is spurious, the Greek is genuine.

literal sense of believing that a proposition is true. Naturally;
for the explicit object is the *word* or *sentences* that Jesus had
just spoken. Similarly John 5:47. Berkhof even allows Acts
16:34, Romans 4:3, and II Timothy 1:12 to mean belief in the
truth of a proposition, although the explicit object of the verb
is *God* or *Christ*.

In spite of these instances, where the predicate is the noun
*God*, though the actual and immediate object is a proposition,
and particularly in contrast with the instances where the object
is explicitly a proposition, Berkhof says, "On the whole this
construction is weaker than the preceding" (p. 494), where
*pisteuo* means "confident trust in a person." But why weaker?
Would it not be more accurate to say that this construction
with a proposition as the object is more literal and accurate
than the preceding abbreviated expressions? Berkhof continues, "In a couple of cases the matter believed hardly rises
into the religious sphere, John 9:18, Acts 9:26 . . . ." But if
these are instances of ordinary usage, and not particularly
religious, such as "The Jews did not believe that he had been
born blind," it should show all the more clearly what the
ordinary meaning of *believing* is. No religious motif is there to
distract one's understanding. It is true that the object of belief
in such instances does not rise into the religious sphere;
sometimes the object may be banal or trivial; but the point at
issue is not the object of belief or faith, but the nature of faith
and the meaning of the verb *pisteuo*.

From page 493 on, Berkhof speaks as follows. *Pistis* (the
noun) and *pisteuein* (the verb) "do not always have exactly the
same meaning." He specifies two meanings of the noun in
classical Greek. "It denotes (a) a conviction based on confidence in a person and in his testimony, which as such is
distinguished from knowledge resting on personal investigation; and (b) the confidence itself on which such a conviction

rests. This is more than a mere intellectual conviction that a person is reliable; it presupposes a personal relation to the object of confidence, a giving out of oneself to rest in another."

The lexical information of this quotation is accurate enough; but the comments are groundless. Why is confidence in a person's truthfulness more than "a *mere* intellectual conviction that a person is reliable" ? What is intended in the pejorative use of the word "mere" ? Why is a conviction of another person's honesty and reliability not a "personal relation" ? And can any intelligible sense be found in the phrase "a giving out of oneself to rest in another" ?

However, to continue the quotations from page 494 on, we read that in the New Testament "the following meanings [of the noun *pistis*] should be distinguished: an intellectual belief or conviction, resting on the testimony of another, and therefore based on trust in this other rather than on personal investigation,[23] Philippians 1:27 [which rather obviously refers to the doctrines of the gospel], II Corinthians 4:13, II Thessalonians 2:13 [the object here is truth] and especially in the writings of John; and (b) a confiding trust or confidence . . . Romans 3:22, 25; 5:1, 2; 9:30, 32. . . . This trust must be distinguished from that on which the intellectual truth mentioned above under (a) above rests."

But why? No reason is given. Is it not true that "a confiding trust or confidence" depends on previous instances of being told the truth? The first time I meet a man and hear him speak—unless he comes already highly recommended, which

---

23. Though it is not necessary to the main argument, one may note that the phrase "rather than on personal investigation" conflicts with actual usage. A scientist personally investigates this or that phenomenon; he accepts a great deal of evidence in favor of a certain hypothesis; and he believes that this equation is the correct explanation. That belief may depend on the testimony of someone we think competent goes without saying; but this condition should not be made a part of the definition of faith.

merely pushes the illustration one step backwards—I cannot reasonably grant him a confiding trust or confidence. After I have observed his habit of always telling the truth, I can have confidence in him. But this is also an intellectual belief that he constantly tells the truth. It differs from the former only in the circumstance that the object of the belief is a different proposition. First, I believed *that* a chemical formula would do so and so; now I believe *that* he always tells the truth.

Berkhof cited some references to support his contention. But Romans 3:22 does not support him. It merely mentions, in four words, "faith in Jesus Christ." The immediately following words are "to all who believe." What they believe is more explicitly stated in 3:25, which Berkhof also lists. The phrase is "through faith in his blood." Clearly this is not baldly literal. *Blood* is a symbol for the Atonement. It cannot even be restricted to Christ's death, for the Pharisees themselves believed that Christ died. What the Pharisees did not believe was the significance of Christ's death, namely, that he paid the penalty of our sin. Verses 25 and 26 are the best summary in the New Testament of the core of the gospel: the doctrine of justification by faith; and this doctrine—a set of propositions—is the object of belief. Nor do Berkhof's other citations (Romans 5:1, 2; 9:30, 32) support his conclusion. They make no distinction such as Berkhof makes. They simply speak of faith. By saying five lines below that "This last [yielding of Christ and trusting in him] is specifically called saving faith," Berkhof implies that the conviction of the truth of the gospel and "intellectual trust" is not saving faith. Romans is a great book, and we are willing to quote it, more than willing, anxious: Romans 10:9 says that "if you confess with your mouth that Jesus is Lord, and believe in your heart that God raised him from the dead, you shall be saved." As the Old Testament has made abundantly clear, the heart is the mind; and believing that God raised Christ from the dead is as intellectual an exercise as believing that two and two are four.

On page 495 Berkhof continues, Faith "is also represented as a hungering and thirsting. . . . In eating and drinking we not only have the conviction that the necessary food and drink is present, but also the confident expectation that it will satisfy us."

There is a major flaw in this paragraph: it misapplies a metaphorical expression. Hungering and thirsting are figures of speech, as is nourishment also. Of course having food present before us does not nourish us. It must be eaten. Now, Berkhof compares the uneaten food before us with believing the gospel. This requires, in the spiritual application of the metaphor, an additional factor beyond believing. A proper application of the metaphor would compare looking at the food before eating it with hearing the gospel before believing it. In neither case is there nourishment. Nourishment comes, literally, when we eat; spiritually when we believe the good news. Understanding the words of the evangelist is an intellectual act and it does not save; believing those words after having understood them saves. But this too is an intellectual act. The objects of propositions are different. The first act, in unbelief, is "I understand that the evangelist thinks Christ died for man's sins." The second act is "I believe that it is true that Christ died for man's sins." These are both cases of intellectual or volitional assent; but the objects, i.e., the propositions, differ immensely.

There are, he says, other instances of the verb *believe* where "the deeper meaning of the word, that of firm trustful reliance, comes to its full rights." But Berkhof, like others, fails to show how this "deeper meaning" differs from the straightforward literal meaning. Among the many instances of the verb *believe*, there is, to repeat, a difference of objects. One may believe that two and two are four and this is arithmetic; one may also believe that asparagus belongs to the lily family, and this is botany. Botany is not mathematics, of course; but the psychology or linguistics of *believe* is identical in all cases. Therefore, one should not confuse an analysis of belief with an analysis of numbers or plants. Christ's promises of salvation are vastly different from the propositions of botany; but believing is always thinking that a proposition is true. The further development will also support this conclusion.

## 16. Person or Proposition?

While Professor Berkhof serves as a good example, many other Protestant theologians also, both Lutheran and Reformed, tend to make a sharp distinction between "a confident resting on a person" and "the assent given to a testimony." "Confident reliance" is supposed to differ from "intellectual assent."

The term *resting* or *reliance* is seldom if ever explained in theology books. One is left in the dark as to what it means. An illustration may furnish a clue and make the words intelligible. Suppose a high school student is assigned a problem in geometry. He works out a solution, looks at it from all angles, perhaps he corrects a small detail and then tests each step again to see if he has made a mistake; seeing none he now puts down his pencil and rests. That is to say, he has assented to his argument. He believes he now has the truth.

But most theologians are not so clear, nor can they, as earlier indicated, bolster up their imagined distinction with references to *pisteuein eis*, for a few paragraphs back Kittel disposed of such a contention. English also has the same usage. As modernism developed in the 1920's and suspicion attached to this or that minister, people would ask, Does he believe in the Virgin Birth, Does he believe in the Atonement? They did not ask, Does he believe the Virgin Birth? The preposition *in* was regularly used. But of course the meaning was, Does he believe *that* the Virgin Birth is true, Does he believe *that* Christ's death was a substitutionary sacrifice? Thus, to believe in a person is to be confident, i.e., to believe that he will continue to tell the truth.

In spite of the popularity and supposed superior spirituality of the contrast between a *mere* intellectual proposition and a *warm*, living person, it rests on a mistaken psychological analysis. Even Berkhof admits, with at least an appearance of inconsistency, that "As a psychological phenomenon, faith in the religious sense does not differ from faith in general. . . . Christian faith in the most comprehensive sense is man's persuasion of the truth of Scripture on the basis of the authority of God" (p. 501).

This is an excellent statement and should be defended against Berkhof's previous contrary assertions.


# 17. The Object

Still a most embarrassing question has not yet been answered, or even asked. It is this: If the object of saving faith is a proposition, what is that proposition? Surely no one is justified by believing that Abraham lived about 2000 B.C., or that Saul was the first King of Israel, though both of these propositions are completely Scriptural. Nor can we as Protestants believe implicitly whatever the Bible says. Calvin put it tersely: implicit faith is ignorance, not knowledge. What one has never heard or read cannot be believed, for faith cometh by hearing. Hearing what? We do not hear or read the whole Bible every day; we cannot remember it, if we read it through once a year. And a recent convert has probably never read it all. Then which verse, of the several an evangelist might quote, is the one which, believed, justifies the sinner? Has any reader of this study ever heard a minister answer or even ask this question?

When this subject was touched on many pages back, it was said that repentance was necessary. "Repent and be baptized" is a well-known command. But it does not answer the present question. To repent is to change one's mind. But in what respect? Beliefs, resolutions, ideas come and go. We are always changing our minds, and obviously there are many changes of mind that have nothing to do with justification. The question presses upon us: which change of mind?

Among the theologians previously quoted, Owen's discussion stimulates this question. Any attentive reader—there are many inattentive—must face the problem. But though the question is so obvious, the answer is not. Indeed, the question has no answer; that is, it has no single answer. Centuries ago a somewhat similar situation and difficulty arose and was given an impossible answer. Years after Athanasius wrote the Nicene Creed, a so-called Athanasian Creed was formulated that pronounced damnation on everyone who did not believe its numerous propositions on the Trinity. The propositions themselves are on the whole very good; but less than one percent of the Christian community can recite them from memory. Possibly not more than twenty-five percent have even heard them. No Calvinist would assert that salvation requires us to believe them explicitly. On the opposite end of the scale from those who would insist on the wording of the Athanasian Creed, some independent churches write their own creed of five or six articles with fewer words than this one article on the Trinity. But are these few the irreducible minimum for salvation? The

question above asks for precisely those beliefs which are necessary for justification.

Consider the case of Justin Martyr, one of the earliest
heroes of the faith. Did he really have saving faith? He was a
Christian, was he not? He died for the name of our Lord and
Savior. He must have been regenerated and justified, must he
not? But it is doubtful that any strong Lutheran or Calvinistic
church would have admitted him even to communicant mem-
bership. His view of the Atonement was abysmal. Quite possibly the strife-torn church in Corinth, troubled with fornica-
tion, law-suits, and idol-worship—its members do not seem to
have denied Christ's resurrection, but they had denied the
resurrection of believers—had a better theology than Justin
Martyr. But to what justifying propositions did he or they
assent?

Now, Justin Martyr was not a moron. Morons have
doubtless been regenerated and justified. Some members of
extremely primitive tribes also, with their minds incredibly
confused. What propositions did they believe? Is there any
passage in Scripture that identifies, in a scale of decreasing
knowledge, the very minimum by which someone can still be
justified?

But even if a minimum of propositions could be listed,
below which number justification were impossible, it would
still be the wrong question with a perverted outlook. This is the
basic weakness contributing to the low spiritual level of most
so-called fundamentalist congregations. The Church is neither
commanded, encouraged, nor even permitted to be satisfied
with a bare minimum of half a dozen doctrines. Historic
Presbyterianism is in a much better position with its multi-
paragraph thirty-three chapters of the Westminster Confession. The Bible commands the maximum, not the minimum.
Jesus said,

Matthew 28:19, 20 Teach all nations . . . instructing them to observe *all whatever* I command you.

There seems to be no other conclusion but that God justifies sinners by means of many combinations of propositions believed. For which reason a minister should not confine himself to topics popularly thought to be "evangelistic," but should preach the whole counsel of God, trusting that God will give someone the gift of faith through sermons on the Trinity, eschatology, or the doctrine of immediate imputation.

## 18. A Conclusion

The sections of this monograph have presented some of the history of the doctrine of faith and have explained a fair amount of its Scriptural basis, along with a few Calvinistic implications. That the drawing of valid implications is justified, the Westminster Confession asserts in I, 6: "The whole counsel of God, concerning all things necessary for his own glory, man's salvation, faith, and life, is either expressly set down in Scripture, or by good and necessary consequence may be deduced from Scripture." Obviously; for otherwise how could any orthodox minister preach a sermon? This dependence on implication, deduction, necessary consequence is indispensable for the propagation of the gospel. Those "religious" people who decry logic lack every basis for proclaiming any message at all. No declarative sentence can have a meaning except in virtue of the law of contradiction. See St. Aristotle, *Metaphysics,* Book Gamma. Or if the *Metaphysics* is not on your night table, read the Gospel and First Epistle of John.

The present theological climate, however, is inimical to clear thinking. Intellectualism is in disgrace. Even such a conservative, orthodox theologian as G.I. Williamson (*The West-*

*minster Confession of Faith,* Presbyterian and Reformed Publishing Co., 1964), though he does not deny the section of the Confession just quoted, passes over the matter of deduction in one sentence (p. 11). He then immediately tries to restrict its application by saying, "The Law of Moses, for example, is not expressed by way of abstract principles. Moses declared the law in terms of concrete instances." This is ridiculous. The Ten Commandments do not include a single concrete case. They forbid all murder: They mention neither Cain nor Lamech. They condemn all adultery: They do not specify any single instance. They prohibit all theft: Rachel's particular example is missing. Of course, Williamson is not consistently opposed to deductive logic. He rather represents those conservative theologians who have not completely escaped the influence of contemporary irrationalism.

By and large, twentieth century religion is irrational and anti-intellectual. The earlier modernism was covertly so; the later humanism, neo-orthodoxy or existentialism are violently so. Anti-intellectualism has no place for Biblical and Calvinistic faith. Scriptural "information," or historical statements as Kierkegaard put it, have nothing to do with salvation; and salvation itself is sometimes reduced to an earthly life minus anxiety. Karl Barth, for example, ridicules the empty tomb and talks vaguely about "the Easter event." Instead of preaching propositions, these men recommend an irrational experience, an encounter, a wager, a confrontation. If anything is to be believed, it is that authentic Christianity is self-contradictory.[24]

This religious neo-orthodoxy is paralleled by atheistic existentialism. And modern culture as a whole is impregnated with Freudian irrationalistic emotionalism. Even if the temper

---

24. *Karl Barth's Theological Method* (Presbyterian and Reformed Pub. Co., 1963). Paul K. Jewett, *Emil Brunner's Concept of Revelation*, James Clarke & Co., 1954.

of the times cannot be altered, maybe a few ministers who want to be orthodox can be shown how much their secular education, not only in the schools but also through the press, has diluted their gospel, and thus be persuaded to return to Calvin and Paul.

Saving faith as assent, truth as propositions (there is no other kind of *truth*), the inerrancy of Scripture, with the outright rejection of all irrationalism, are integral parts of a single system.

On one or the other of these several points, consider Calvin once more.

In his *Commentary* on John 3:33 Calvin wrote, ". . . giving their assent to God . . . To *believe* the Gospel is nothing else than to *assent* to the *truths* which God has revealed."

On John 6:40 he says, "That man offers an aggravated insult to the Holy Ghost, who refuses to *assent* to his simple testimony . . . Faith proceeds from the *knowledge* of Christ."

At John 6:69 we read, ". . . we *believe* and *know* . . . Faith itself is truly the eye of the *understanding* . . . *Knowledge* is connected with faith because we are certain and fully convinced of the *truth* of God."

Then on John 17:8, "Nothing which relates to God can be known aright but by faith, but in faith there is such certainty that it is justly called *knowledge*."

Commenting on Ephesians 4:13, which states the goal of a unity of faith and a mature knowledge of the Son of God, Calvin teaches that "Enthusiasts [Pentecostals et al.] dream that the use of the ministry ceases as soon as we have been led to Christ [because we can now depend on guidance and visions]. . . . Paul maintains that we must persevere . . . make progress till death . . . that we must not be ashamed to be the scholars of the church, to which Christ has committed our education." The epistle and the commentary continue by warning us not to remain children, deceived by every wind of false and deceitful doctrine, but to become mature.

Note too how maturity is described in Hebrews 5:11—6:2. The babe in Christ, who has been nourished on milk, must now eat solid food and become a teacher. The doctrines of repentance and faith, of baptism and ordination, of the resurrection and the final judgment, are elementary. One must press on to the maturity of more complex theology: namely, all three volumes of Hodge.

Foundational to this intellectualism, this rationalism, or however anyone wishes to name this emphasis on truth, is the doctrine that man is the image of God. One should not try to dilute this doctrine by picturing man as a container somewhere within which the image of God may be found. I Corinthians 11:7 does not say that man *has* the image of God; it says that man *is* the image of God. This image, which distinguishes man from animals, is rationality. It was not destroyed by the fall, for we are still human beings and not animals. We are still generically rational, though sin has considerably damaged our use of reason. We add up our check stubs incorrectly, and our emotions drive us into foolish conduct (or worse). But we are still human because we are the created image of God. Though we often believe falsehoods, we are still obligated to believe the truth. And if God causes us to believe, since faith is the gift of God, then we are slowly renewed in the knowledge and righteousness of our original creation.

Incidentally, this is a further reason for rejecting the empirical epistemology of Thomas and some Protestants. Adam was created, having knowledge. The Thomists go so far as to say that Paul in the first chapter of Romans placed his stamp of approval on empiricism and the cosmological argument. There is a different interpretation of chapter one; but Romans 2:15 is a sufficient refutation of the *tabula rasa* theory.

In the split second of his creation, Adam, before he could rub his eyes and see the sun, had a knowledge of God, and of logic too.

If any reader is disturbed by the present author's insistence on logic, reason, intellect, and knowledge in comparison with his lack of emphasis on righteousness, it should be remembered that (1) there can be no righteousness without knowledge, (2) American evangelicalism puts most of its emphasis on conduct, morality, the fruits of the Spirit, and "practical" Christianity, (3) there is a woeful lack of emphasis on truth, theology, the teachings of Scripture. Of course these teachings have moral implications, but the righteousness enjoined in Romans 12-15 plus some in chapter 16 has as its foundation the eleven preceding chapters. Does it not follow therefore that a minister should preach eleven sermons on deep doctrine to every six or five and a half on conduct? The latter should by no means be omitted: The crime and depravity of American society is without parallel in history since the time of the Roman Empire. Nor has the Church itself much to be proud of. But a one-sided preaching of righteousness will have little effect on Las Vegas or New York. Not until this alcoholic, drug-ridden scum hears and believes—faith cometh by hearing, not by mystic encounters—hears and believes the doctrines of the Trinity, the Incarnation, the Atonement, Justification by faith, and the Second Advent, will there be any moral improvement. It is Justification that produces Sanctification, and Justification occurs by means of faith.

The present writer, I hope evidently, does not disparage righteousness; but the topic of the monograph is faith, and to the main conclusion the argument now returns.

The most common analysis of personality among conservative Christians today is the three-fold division into intellect, will, and emotions. As a matter of fact, a two-fold division into intellect and emotion is probably more common, for a Freudian, sexually-oriented society has discarded the will. It was not always so. Whedon's *The Freedom of the Will* was published in 1864; Girardeau's *The Will in its Theological Relations* was published in 1891; and in 1898 came Archibald Alexander's *Theories of the Will*. The first two are Arminian, and no doubt Arminians, if asked, will still assert the freedom of the will, but you have to ask them; for the Nazarenes, the Pentecostals, the Holiness groups give me the impression of having forgotten the will in their constant stress of emotion. Henry B. Smith, a Calvinist of last century (*System of Christian Theology*, New York, 1884, p. 540) divided "the whole soul" into intellect, will, and sensibilities. Strange, even the empirical theologians of today hardly ever mention sensation in this connection, however much they make use of it in epistemology.

A paragraph on Augustine will prove profitable. Since he thought of man as a replica of the Trinity, he needed a threefold division, but he did not always come up with the same three. Sometimes it was *mens, notitia,* and *amor* (mind, knowledge, and love); more frequently it was *memoria*—Augustine defended the continuity of the resurrected saint with his earthly life on the basis of a continuing memory—*intelligentia*, and *voluntas*. He also enumerated *memoria* (not of oneself, as above, but "memory" of God), *intelligentia*, and *amor*.

Those who know little about the Bible and less about the history of theology will delightedly grasp at Augustine's love, with the remark, "There you have emotion, and the Bible surely says a lot about love." In answer, one must admit that Augustine not only stressed love, but even placed it in a position superior to intellect. But the love Augustine had in mind, and love as considered in Scripture, is a volition, not an emotion. The Scripture commands love. Commands are addressed to the will. Emotions are involuntary. One should not interpret, misinterpret, Scriptural love in terms of the secular psychology of the twentieth century. God has no emotions, and his image, man, in his unfallen state, may have been analyzed into intellect, and will, knowledge and righteousness. Emotion and disease came in with the fall.

Earlier in this century J. Gresham Machen defended, and suffered for, the primacy of the intellect. "To the pragmatic skepticism of the modern religious world, therefore, the Bible is sharply opposed; against the passionate anti-intellectualism of a large part of the modern Church it maintains the primacy of the intellect; it teaches plainly that God has given to man a faculty of reason which is capable of apprehending truth, even truth about God" (*What is Faith*, p. 51; The Macmillan Co., 1925).

To summarize a few thoughts from his introductory chapter is not so much plagiarism as a recommendation that the population of this ninth decade return and read this classic of the third.

Machen begins by noting that some devout souls regard an analysis of faith as "impertinent and unnecessary. Faith . . . cannot be known except by experience, and . . . logical analysis of it . . . will only serve to destroy its power and charm. . . . Religion is an ineffable experience; the intellectual expression of it . . . theology may vary and yet religion may remain the same" (p. 13). Those who entertain this view avoid defining their terms. "They are greatly incensed when they are asked to tell in simple language what they mean by these terms (atonement, redemption, faith). They find it "disconcerting to be asked what faith is" (p. 14).

The same anti-intellectualism is evident in secular education also. Machen lived before the invention of the phrase, "Johnny can't read;" but he could say, "The undergraduate student of the present day is being told that . . . the exercise of memory is a rather childish and mechanical thing, and that what he is really in college to do is to think for himself and to unify his world." Later this phrase became "to do one's own thing.""He usually made a poor business of unifying his world, and the reason is clear . . . he has no world to unify. He has not acquired a knowledge of a sufficient number of facts in order even to learn the method of putting facts together" (p. 16). "A mass of details stored up in the mind does not in itself make a thinker; but on the other hand thinking is absolutely impossible without the mass of details. . . . It is impossible to think with an empty mind" (p. 20).

The decline of intellectualism, if "lamentable in secular education, is tenfold worse in the sphere of the Christian religion. . . . Bible classes today often avoid a study of the actual contents of the Bible as they would avoid pestilence or disease; to many persons in the Church the notion of getting the simple historical contents of the Bible straight in mind is an entirely new idea" (p. 20-21).

In addition to secular education and the Church, anti-intellectualism has invaded the Christian home. "I did not get my knowledge of the Bible from Sunday School, but . . . [from] my mother at home. And I will venture to say that although my mental ability was certainly of no extraordinary kind [a statement proved false by his extraordinarily competent publications] I had a better knowledge of the Bible at fourteen years of age than is possessed by many students in the theological seminaries of the present day" (p. 22). The present writer too memorized the Shorter Catechism by that age. But "the lamentable fact is that the Christian home [two exceptions are my daughters and their children] as an educational institution, has largely ceased to function." Now fifty years later, home and family have been largely aborted. This educational, religious, and moral decline, Machen attributes to anti-intellectualism.

He gives an example—Goodspeed's mistranslation of the verb *dikaioō*. Another example is Ellwood's perversion of history by saying that "Jesus concerned himself but little with the question of existence after death."

Then Machen states his purpose for writing his book: "As over against this anti-intellectual tendency in the modern world, it will be one chief purpose of the present little book to defend the primacy of the intellect, and in particular to try to break down the false and disastrous opposition which has been set up between knowledge and faith" (p. 26). This introductory chapter continues for another twenty pages, but these excerpts form a sufficient recommendation that the book be read again.

Let other books detail the humanistic degradation of the public schools under the National Education Association; let the pastors point out the anti-christian bigotry of the present Secretary of the federal Department of Education; let a Moral Majority mount an attack on corrupt and prodigal congressmen. In the study at hand the subject is saving faith.

Faith, by definition, is assent to understood propositions. Not all cases of assent, even assent to Biblical propositions, are saving faith; but all saving faith is assent to one or more Biblical propositions.

# Scripture Index

# Index

# The Crisis of Our Time

Historians have christened the thirteenth century the Age of Faith and termed the eighteenth century the Age of Reason. The twentieth century has been called many things: the Atomic Age, the Age of Inflation, the Age of the Tyrant, the Age of Aquarius. But it deserves one name more than the others: the Age of Irrationalism. Contemporary secular intellectuals are anti-intellectual. Contemporary philosophers are anti-philosophy. Contemporary theologians are anti-theology.

In past centuries secular philosophers have generally believed that knowledge is possible to man. Consequently they expended a great deal of thought and effort trying to justify knowledge. In the twentieth century, however, the optimism of the secular philosophers has all but disappeared. They despair of knowledge.

Like their secular counterparts, the great theologians and doctors of the church taught that knowledge is possible to man. Yet the theologians of the twentieth century have repudiated that belief. They also despair of knowledge. This radical skepticism has filtered down from the philosophers and theologians and penetrated our entire culture, from television to music to literature. *The Christian in the twentieth century is confronted with an overwhelming cultural consensus—sometimes stated*

133

*explicitly, but most often implicitly: Man does not and cannot know anything truly.*

What does this have to do with Christianity? Simply this: If man can know nothing truly, man can truly know nothing. We cannot know that the Bible is the Word of God, that Christ died for sin, or that Christ is alive today at the right hand of the Father. Unless knowledge is possible, Christianity is nonsensical, for it claims to be knowledge. What is at stake in the twentieth century is not simply a single doctrine, such as the Virgin Birth, or the existence of hell, as important as those doctrines may be, but the whole of Christianity itself. If knowledge is not possible to man, it is worse than silly to argue points of doctrine—it is insane.

The irrationalism of the present age is so thorough-going and pervasive that even the Remnant—the segment of the professing church that remains faithful—has accepted much of it, frequently without even being aware of what it was accepting. In some circles this irrationalism has become synonymous with piety and humility, and those who oppose it are denounced as rationalists—as though to be logical were a sin. Our contemporary anti-theologians make a contradiction and call it a Mystery. The faithful ask for truth and are given Paradox. If any balk at swallowing the absurdities of the anti-theologians, they are frequently marked as heretics or schismatics who seek to act independently of God.

There is no greater threat facing the true Church of Christ at this moment than the irrationalism that now controls our entire culture. Communism, guilty of tens of millions of murders, including those of millions of Christians, is to be feared, but not nearly so much as the idea that we do not and cannot know the truth. Hedonism, the popular philosophy of America, is not to be feared so much as the belief that logic —that "mere human logic," to use the religious irrationalists' own phrase—is futile. The attacks on truth, on revelation, on the intellect, and on logic are renewed daily. But note well: The misologists—the haters of logic—use logic to demonstrate the futility of using logic. The anti-intellectuals construct intricate intellectual arguments to prove the insufficiency of the intellect. The anti-theologians use the revealed Word of God to show that there can be no revealed Word of God—or that if there could, it would remain impenetrable darkness and Mystery to our finite minds.

## Nonsense Has Come

Is it any wonder that the world is grasping at straws—the straws of experientialism, mysticism and drugs? After all, if people are told that the Bible contains insoluble mysteries, then is not a flight into mysticism to be expected? On what grounds can it be condemned? Certainly not on logical grounds or Biblical grounds, if logic is futile and the Bible unintelligible. Moreover, if it cannot be condemned on logical or Biblical grounds, it cannot be condemned at all. If people are going to have a religion of the mysterious, they will not adopt Christianity: They will have a genuine mystery religion. "Those who call for Nonsense," C.S. Lewis once wrote, "will find that it comes." And that is precisely what has happened. The popularity of Eastern mysticism, of drugs, and of religious experience is the logical consequence of the irrationalism of the twentieth century. There can and will be no Christian revival—and no reconstruction of society—unless and until the irrationalism of the age is totally repudiated by Christians.

## The Church Defenseless

Yet how shall they do it? The spokesmen for Christianity

have been fatally infected with irrationalism. The seminaries, which annually train thousands of men to teach millions of Christians, are the finishing schools of irrationalism, completing the job begun by the government schools and colleges. Some of the pulpits of the most conservative churches (we are not speaking of the apostate churches) are occupied by graduates of the anti-theological schools. These products of modern anti-theological education, when asked to give a reason for the hope that is in them, can generally respond with only the intellectual analogue of a shrug—a mumble about Mystery. They have not grasped—and therefore cannot teach those for whom they are responsible—the first truth: "And ye shall know the truth." Many, in fact, explicitly deny it, saying that, at best, we possess only "pointers" to the truth, or something "similar" to the truth, a mere analogy. Is the impotence of the Christian Church a puzzle? Is the fascination with pentecostalism and faith healing among members of conservative churches an enigma? Not when one understands the sort of studied nonsense that is purveyed in the name of God in the seminaries.

## The Trinity Foundation

The creators of The Trinity Foundation firmly believe that theology is too important to be left to the licensed theologians—the graduates of the schools of theology. They have created The Trinity Foundation for the express purpose of teaching the faithful all that the Scriptures contain—not warmed over, baptized, secular philosophies. Each member of the board of directors of The Trinity Foundation has signed this oath: "I believe that the Bible alone and the Bible in its entirety is the Word of God and, therefore, inerrant in the autographs. I believe that the system of truth presented in the Bible is best summarized in the Westminster Confession of Faith. So help me God."

The ministry of The Trinity Foundation is the presentation of the system of truth taught in Scripture as clearly and as completely as possible. We do not regard obscurity as a virtue, nor confusion as a sign of spirituality. Confusion, like all error, is sin, and teaching that confusion is all that Christians can hope for is doubly sin.

The presentation of the truth of Scripture necessarily involves the rejection of error. The Foundation has exposed and will continue to expose the irrationalism of the twentieth century, whether its current spokesman be an existentialist philosopher or a professed Reformed theologian. We oppose anti-intellectualism, whether it be espoused by a neo-orthodox theologian or a fundamentalist evangelist. We reject misology, whether it be on the lips of a neo-evangelical or those of a Roman Catholic charismatic. To each error we bring the brilliant light of Scripture, proving all things, and holding fast to that which is true.

## The Primacy of Theory

The ministry of The Trinity Foundation is not a "practical" ministry. If you are a pastor, we will not enlighten you on how to organize an ecumenical prayer meeting in your community or how to double church attendance in a year. If you are a homemaker, you will have to read elsewhere to find out how to become a total woman. If you are a businessman, we will not tell you how to develop a social conscience. The professing church is drowning in such "practical" advice.

The Trinity Foundation is unapologetically theoretical in its outlook, believing that theory without practice is dead, and that practice without theory is blind. The trouble with the

professing church is not primarily in its practice, but in its
theory. Christians do not know, and many do not even care to
know, the doctrines of Scripture. Doctrine is intellectual, and
Christians are generally anti-intellectual. Doctrine is ivory
tower philosophy, and they scorn ivory towers. The ivory tower,
however, is the control tower of a civilization. It is a fundamental, theoretical mistake of the practical men to think that they
can be merely practical, for practice is always the practice of
some theory. The relationship between theory and practice is
the relationship between cause and effect. If a person believes
correct theory, his practice will tend to be correct. The practice
of contemporary Christians is immoral because it is the practice
of false theories. It is a major theoretical mistake of the
practical men to think that they can ignore the ivory towers of
the philosophers and theologians as irrelevant to their lives.
Every action that the "practical" men take is governed by the
thinking that has occurred in some ivory tower—whether that
tower be the British Museum, the Academy, a home in Basel,
Switzerland, or a tent in Israel.

## In Understanding Be Men

It is the first duty of the Christian to understand correct
theory—correct doctrine—and thereby implement correct
practice. This order—first theory, then practice—is both logical
and Biblical. It is, for example, exhibited in Paul's epistle to the
Romans, in which he spends the first eleven chapters expound-
ing theory and the last five discussing practice. The contemporary teachers of Christians have not only reversed the order, they
have inverted the Pauline emphasis on theory and practice. The
virtually complete failure of the teachers of the professing
church to instruct the faithful in correct doctrine is the cause of
the misconduct and cultural impotence of Christians. The

Church's lack of power is the result of its lack of truth. The *Gospel* is the power of God, not religious experience or personal relationship. The Church has no power because it has abandoned the Gospel, the good news, for a religion of experientialism. Twentieth century American Christians are children carried about by every wind of doctrine, not knowing what they believe, or even if they believe anything for certain.

The chief purpose of The Trinity Foundation is to counteract the irrationalism of the age and to expose the errors of the teachers of the church. Our emphasis—on the Bible as the sole source of truth, on the primacy of the intellect, on the supreme importance of correct doctrine, and on the necessity for systematic and logical thinking—is almost unique in Christendom. To the extent that the church survives—and she will survive and flourish—it will be because of her increasing acceptance of these basic ideas and their logical implications.

We believe that the Trinity Foundation is filling a vacuum in Christendom. We are saying that Christianity is intellectually defensible—that, in fact, it is the only intellectually defensible system of thought. We are saying that God has made the wisdom of this world—whether that wisdom be called science, religion, philosophy, or common sense—foolishness. We are appealing to all Christians who have not conceded defeat in the intellectual battle with the world to join us in our efforts to raise a standard to which all men of sound mind can repair.

The love of truth, of God's Word, has all but disappeared in our time. We are committed to and pray for a great instauration. But though we may not see this reformation of Christendom in our lifetimes, we believe it is our duty to present the whole counsel of God because Christ has commanded it. The results of our teaching are in God's hands, not ours. Whatever those results, His Word is never taught in vain, but always accomplishes the result that He intended it to accomplish. Professor Gordon H. Clark has stated our view well:

There have been times in the history of God's people, for example, in the days of Jeremiah, when refreshing grace and widespread revival were not to be expected: the time was one of chastisement. If this twentieth century is of a similar nature, individual Christians here and there can find comfort and strength in a study of God's Word. But if God has decreed happier days for us and if we may expect a world-shaking and genuine spiritual awakening, then it is the author's belief that a zeal for souls, however necessary, is not the sufficient condition. Have there not been devout saints in every age, numerous enough to carry on a revival? Twelve such persons are plenty. What distinguishes the arid ages from the period of the Reformation, when nations were moved as they had not been since Paul preached in Ephesus, Corinth, and Rome, is the latter's fullness of knowledge of God's Word. To echo an early Reformation thought, when the ploughman and the garage attendant know the Bible as well as the theologian does, and know it better than some contemporary theologians, then the desired awakening shall have already occurred.

In addition to publishing books, of which *Faith and Saving Faith* is the fifth, the Foundation publishes a bimonthly newsletter, *The Trinity Review*. Subscriptions to *The Review* are free; please write to the address below to become a subscriber. If you would like further information or would like to join us in our work, please let us know.

The Trinity Foundation is a non-profit foundation tax-exempt under section 501 (c)(3) of the Internal Revenue Code of 1954. You can help us disseminate the Word of God through your tax-deductible contributions to the Foundation.

*And we know that the Son of God is come, and hath given us an understanding, that we may know him that is true, and we are in him that is true, in his Son Jesus Christ. This is the true God, and eternal life.*

John W. Robbins
President

# Intellectual Ammunition

The Trinity Foundation is committed to the reconstruction of philosophy and theology along Biblical lines. We regard God's command to bring all our thoughts into conformity with Christ very seriously, and the books listed below are designed to accomplish that goal. They are written with two subordinate purposes: (1) to demolish all secular claims to knowledge; and (2) to build a system of truth based upon the Bible alone.

## Works of Philosophy

**Behaviorism and Christianity**, Gordon H. Clark                    $5.95

Behaviorism *is a critique of both secular and religious behaviorists. It includes chapters on John Watson, Edgar S. Singer Jr., Gilbert Ryle, B.F. Skinner, and Donald MacKay. Clark's refutation of behaviorism and his argument for a Christian doctrine of man are unanswerable.*

**A Christian Philosophy of Education**, Gordon H. Clark             $8.95

*The first edition of this book was published in 1946. It sparked the contemporary interest in Christian schools. Dr. Clark has thoroughly revised and updated it, and it is needed now more than ever. Its chapters include: The Need for a World-View, The Christian World-View, The Alternative to Christian Theism, Neutrality, Ethics, The Christian*

*Philosophy of Education, Academic Matters, Kindergarten to University.
Three appendices are included as well: The Relationship of Public
Education to Christianity, A Protestant World-View, and Art and the
Gospel.*

**A Christian View of Men and Things**, Gordon H. Clark          $8.95
*No other book achieves what* A Christian View *does: the
presentation of Christianity as it applies to history, politics, ethics,
science, religion, and epistemology. Clark's command of both worldly
philosophy and Scripture is evident on every page, and the result is a
breathtaking and invigorating challenge to the wisdom of this world.*

**Clark Speaks From The Grave**, Gordon H. Clark                $3.95
*Dr. Clark chides some of his critics for their failure to defend
Christianity competently.* Clark Speaks *is a stimulating and illuminating
discussion of the errors of contemporary apologists.*

**Dewey,** Gordon H. Clark                                      $2.00
*Dewey has had an immense influence on American philosophy and
education. His irrationalism, the effects of which we can see in
government education, is thoroughly criticized by Clark.*

**Education, Christianity, and the State**                      $7.95
J. Gresham Machen
*Machen was one of the foremost educators, theologians, and
defenders of Christianity in the twentieth century. The author of
numerous scholarly books, Machen saw clearly that if Christianity is to
survive and flourish, a system of Christian grade schools must be
established. This collection of essays captures his thought on education
over nearly three decades.*

**Gordon H. Clark: Personal Recollections,**                   $6.95
John W. Robbins, editor
*Friends of Dr. Clark have written their recollections of the man.
Contributors include family members, colleagues, students, and friends*

*such as Harold Lindsell, Carl Henry, Ronald Nash, Dwight Zeller, and Mary Crumpacker. The book includes an extensive bibliography of Clark's work.*

**Logic**, Gordon H. Clark                                          $8.95
*Written as a textbook for Christian schools,* Logic *is another unique book from Clark's pen. His presentation of the laws of thought, which must be followed if Scripture is to be understood correctly, and which are found in Scripture itself, is both clear and thorough.* Logic *is an indispensable book for the thinking Christian.*

**The Philosophy of Science and Belief in God**                     $5.95
Gordon H. Clark
*In opposing the contemporary idolatry of science, Clark analyzes three major aspects of science: the problem of motion, Newtonian science, and modern theories of physics. His conclusion is that science, while it may be useful, is always false; and he demonstrates its falsity in numerous ways. Since science is always false, it can offer no objection to the Bible and Christianity.*

**Religion, Reason and Revelation**, Gordon H. Clark               $7.95
*One of Clark's apologetical masterpieces,* Religion, Reason and Revelation *has been praised for the clarity of its thought and language. It includes chapters on Is Christianity a Religion? Faith and Reason, Inspiration and Language, Revelation and Morality, and God and Evil. It is must reading for all serious Christians.*

**Thales to Dewey: A History of Philosophy,**            paper $11.95
Gordon H. Clark                                        hardback $16.95
*This volume is the best one volume history of philosophy in English.*

**Three Types of Religious Philosophy,** Gordon H. Clark           $6.95
*In this book on apologetics, Clark examines empiricism, rationalism, dogmatism, and contemporary irrationalism, which does not rise to*

*the level of philosophy. He offers a solution to the question, "How can Christianity be defended before the world?"*

# Works of Theology

**The Atonement**, Gordon H. Clark                    $8.95
*This is a major addition to Clark's multi-volume systematic theology. In* The Atonement, *Clark discusses the Covenants, the Virgin Birth and Incarnation, federal headship and representation, the relationship between God's sovereignty and justice, and much more. He analyzes traditional views of the Atonement and criticizes them in the light of Scripture alone.*

**The Biblical Doctrine of Man**, Gordon H. Clark          $5.95
*Is man soul and body or soul, spirit, and body? What is the image of God? Is Adam's sin imputed to his children? Is evolution true? Are men totally depraved? What is the heart? These are some to the questions discussed and answered from Scripture in this book.*

**Cornelius Van Til: The Man and The Myth**               $2.45
John W. Robbins
*The actual teachings of this eminent Philadelphia theologian have been obscured by the myths that surround him. This book penetrates those myths and criticizes Van Til's surprisingly unorthodox views of God and the Bible.*

**Faith and Saving Faith**, Gordon H. Clark               $6.95
*The views of the Roman Catholic church, John Calvin, Thomas Manton, John Owen, Charles Hodge, and B.B. Warfield are discussed in this book. Is the object of faith a person or a proposition? Is faith more than belief? Is belief more than thinking with assent, as Augustine said? In a world chaotic with differing views of faith, Clark clearly explains the Biblical view of faith and saving faith.*

**God's Hammer: The Bible and Its Critics**, Gordon H. Clark     $6.95
*The starting point of Christianity, the doctrine on which all other doctrines depend, is "The Bible alone is the Word of God written, and therefore inerrant in the autographs." Over the centuries the opponents of Christianity, with Satanic shrewdness, have concentrated their attacks on the truthfulness and completeness of the Bible. In the twentieth century the attack is not so much in the fields of history and archaeology as in philosophy. Clark's brilliant defense of the complete truthfulness of the Bible is captured in this collection of eleven major essays.*

**The Incarnation,** Gordon H. Clark                             $8.95
*Who was Christ? The attack on the Incarnation in the nineteenth and twentieth centuries has been vigorous, but the orthodox response has been lame. Clark reconstructs the doctrine of the Incarnation building upon and improving upon the Chalcedonian definition.*

**In Defense of Theology**, Gordon H. Clark                     $12.95
*There are four groups to whom Clark addresses this book: the average Christians who are uninterested in theology, the atheists and agnostics, the religious experientalists, and the serious Christians. The vindication of the knowledge of God against the objections of three of these groups is the first step in theology.*

**The Johannine Logos,** Gordon H. Clark                        $5.95
*Clark analyzes the relationship between Christ, who is the truth, and the Bible. He explains why John used the same word to refer to both Christ and his teaching. Chapters deal with the prologue to John's Gospel, Logos and Rheemata, Truth, and Saving Faith.*

**Logical Criticisms of Textual Criticism**, Gordon H. Clark     $2.95
*In this critique of the science of textual criticism, Dr. Clark exposes the fallacious argumentation of the modern textual critics and defends the view that the early Christians knew better than the modern critics which manuscripts of the New Testament were more accurate.*

**Pat Robertson: A Warning to America**, John W. Robbins        $6.95
   *The Protestant Reformation was based on the Biblical principle that the Bible is the only revelation from God, yet a growing political-religious movement, led by Pat Robertson, asserts that God speaks to them directly. This book addresses the serious issue of religious fanaticism in America by examining the theological views of Pat Robertson.*

**Predestination**, Gordon H. Clark                              $7.95
   *Clark thoroughly discusses one of the most controversial and pervasive doctrines of the Bible: that God is, quite literally, Almighty. Free will, the origin of evil, God's omniscience, creation, and the new birth are all presented within a Scriptural framework. The objections of those who do not believe in the Almighty God are considered and refuted. This edition also contains the text of the booklet,* Predestination in the Old Testament.

**Scripture Twisting in the Seminaries. Part 1: Feminism**        $5.95
John W. Robbins
   *An analysis of the views of three graduates of Westminster Seminary on the role of women in the church.*

**The Trinity**, Gordon H. Clark                                 $8.95
   *Apart from the doctrine of Scripture, no teaching of the Bible is more important than the doctrine of God. Clark's defense of the orthodox doctrine of the Trinity is a principal portion of a major new work of Systematic Theology now in progress. There are chapters on the deity of Christ, Augustine, the incomprehensibility of God, Bavinck and Van Til, and the Holy Spirit, among others.*

**What Do Presbyterians Believe?** Gordon H. Clark               $7.95
   *This classic introduction to Christian doctrine has been republished. It is the best commentary on the Westminster Confession of Faith that has ever been written.*

## Commentaries on the New Testament

| | |
|---|---|
| **Colossians,** Gordon H. Clark | $6.95 |
| **Ephesians**, Gordon H. Clark | $8.95 |
| **First and Second Thessalonians**, Gordon H. Clark | $5.95 |
| **The Pastoral Epistles** (I and II Timothy and Titus) | $9.95 |
|    Gordon H. Clark | |

   *All of Clark's commentaries are expository, not technical, and are written for the Christian layman. His purpose is to explain the text clearly and accurately so that the Word of God will be thoroughly known by every Christian. Revivals of Christianity come only through the spread of God's truth. The sound exposition of the Bible, through preaching and through commentaries on Scripture, is the only method of spreading that truth.*

# The Trinity Review

   *The Foundation's bimonthly newsletter,* The Trinity Review, *has been published since 1979 and has carried more than seventy major essays by Gordon H. Clark, J. Gresham Machen, Fyodor Dostoyevsky, Charles Hodge, John Witherspoon, and others. Back issues are available for 40¢ each.*

# The Trinity Library

   *We will send you one copy of each of the 30 books listed above for the low price of $150. The regular price of these books is $218. Or you may order the books you want individually on the order blank on the next page. Because some of the books are in short supply, we must reserve the right to substitute others of equal or greater value in The Trinity Library.*

   *Thank you for your attention. We hope to hear from you soon. This special offer expires June 30, 1992.*

# Order Form

Name _____

Address _____

_____

Please:  ☐ add my name to the mailing list for *The Trinity Review.* I
           understand that there is no charge for the *Review.*

         ☐ accept my tax deductible contribution of $ _____
           for the work of the Foundation.

         ☐ send me _____ copies of *Faith and Saving Faith.*
           I enclose as payment $ _____.

         ☐ send me the Trinity Library of 30 books. I enclose $150 as
           full payment for it.

         ☐ send me the following books. I enclose full payment in the
           amount of $ _____ for them.

_____

_____

_____

_____

_____

_____

_____

Mail to:            The Trinity Foundation
                    Post Office Box 700
                    Jefferson, MD 21755

Please add $1.00 for postage on orders less than $10. Thank you.
For quantity discounts, please write to the Foundation.